FROM THE
GUTTER
TO THE
PULPIT

To Russell

Pastor Billy C. Moore

FROM THE
GUTTER
TO THE
PULPIT

by Billy C. Moore
and Wynell Brooks Hutson

TATE PUBLISHING & *Enterprises*

Published by Tate Publishing & Enterprises, LLC
127 E. Trade Center Terrace | Mustang, Oklahoma 73064 USA
1.888.361.9473 | www.tatepublishing.com

Tate Publishing is committed to excellence in the publishing industry. The company reflects the philosophy established by the founders, based on Psalm 68:11,
"The Lord gave the word and great was the company of
those who published it."

Book design copyright © 2007 by Tate Publishing, LLC. All rights reserved.
Cover design by Jacob Crissup
Interior design by Leah LeFlore

Published in the United States of America

ISBN: 978-1-60247-578-6
1. Religion: Christianity, Inspirational, Protestant
2. Inspiration: Motivational, Autobiography & Biography
07.08.16

Acknowledgments

I must acknowledge it was my dear mother's amazing faith and her unending prayers that kept the blood of Jesus over me as I traveled the road of sin the first forty years of my life. She never wavered in her belief that one day God would honor and answer her prayers.

Honor and thanks are also due to my wife, Ruby, for her love and patience through the rough and rocky first years of our marriage. I hereby recognize the love she manifested toward my mother and my children, Billy, Brenda, and Joe. I commend her on her raising of our son, Bill, who is now Dr. William Moore, pastor of the Living Way Family Church in Brownsville, Texas.

I take this opportunity to acknowledge how God brought together—not by coincidence—a person who had written a book honoring the Lord Jesus, another who had the technical skills to get it to a publisher, and one whom the Lord had told twenty years ago to write his life story—and even gave the story a name.

I express my deep gratitude to Wynell Brooks Hutson (author of *Assignment Precious Cargo*) and Phyllis Hutson, the team who transformed my words into this book you are now holding in your hands.

God used us all. God bless the result.

Contents

Foreword

This book is not for everybody.

This book is not for people who live quiet orderly lives with everything neatly in place—unless underneath all that order is a quiet desperation of hidden chaos.

This book is not for those who wish to engage in philosophical debates about the reality of God and His presence in the world today—unless that debate stems from a desperate desire for reality.

This book is not for theologians who merely wish to debate the efficacy of grace—unless that theologian is hungry for the reality of the power of this grace.

This book is not for people with messed up lives seeking an excuse to continue that lifestyle by blaming people or circumstances. "After all," they say, "it's not really my fault."

This book is not a theological, philosophical, psychological, feel-good excuse to continue wasting life in the gutter.

This book is not for everyone and anyone who isn't desperately seeking real, honest, powerful, unfailing answers to the questions that bedevil us all. Who am I? Why am I here? Where am I going? How do I change things? Who can I really trust? Will anyone "never let me down, fail me or forsake me?" Does anyone really love me just the way I am?

This book is not for everybody. **But it could be exactly what you've been looking for.** You may not want to go all the way to the pulpit, but you desperately want out of the gutter, whether it's lined with gold or garbage. If you're honestly looking for *the* answer to life, then **this book is definitely for you.**

Ben Kinchlow
International Broadcaster, Former Co-host of
700 Club, and Founder of Americans for Israel

A Child of the Depression

Foolishness is bound in the heart of a child…
Proverbs 22:15

He shoved the barrel of the ancient shotgun into my scrawny belly. It didn't have a trigger; you had to pull the hammer back and when you let it go, it would bust the cap and the gun would fire.

He was laughing as he told the other boys, "I am going to shoot Bill."

I gripped the gun at the end of the barrel and moved it aside just as he let his finger slip off the hammer.

The blast blew a hole in a window, went through the house, and broke out another window.

I was eleven years old; death came very near.

When I was twenty-six and working for an electric company, death came even closer. It was drizzling rain and I was up on a pole. I still had my gloves on. I climbed a little higher and took the 4,160 volt line in my hand to lift it over the kingpin and leaned back, forgetting the 2,300 volt line was behind me.

The back of my neck touched the bare wire. The electricity went through my body and came out my left hip, but my life was spared once again.

These are but two perilous instances that happened to me. I believe my life was spared because God had a purpose for me, and He answered my spirit-filled mother's faithful prayers to bring me through many dangers to the place where he could use me.

My mother's entire family was spirit-filled. They attended an Assembly of God church, but she had been removed and told she was on her way to hell because she "bobbed" her hair.

When I was an infant, she was so determined to have me dedicated to the Lord, that she sought out the pastor and begged him to perform the dedication.

He finally agreed that, if she would bring me to his home, he would do it there. She told me that she took me to his house, but he would not allow her to come in. He opened the front door, held the screen door open with his foot, and said the prayer over me.

Quite an inauspicious beginning—a woman of lesser faith would have long since given up and turned bitter.

On October 29, 1929, the stock market crashed. The Great Depression hit our country. Factories closed; mills and mines were abandoned; fortunes were lost. Business and labor were both in serious trouble.

It is said that if you did not live through that time, there is no way you can comprehend how terrible it was. There seemed to be no hope.

I was born in Houston, Texas, on November 24, 1929,

almost at the beginning of this disastrous time in our country. My dad worked in construction, and construction came to a halt.

One can only guess what happened in the hearts of proud men who were accustomed to providing for their families. From the East Coast to the West Coast men went looking for jobs, but jobs were hard to find.

Eighteen months after I was born, my father also went looking for a job. He walked away from my mother and me. We never heard from him again.

I don't remember my father. My mother never told me anything about him and I never questioned her. For years I thought I might be illegitimate. Since my mother had no other place to go when my father left, we moved in with her parents. I looked upon my Grampa as my dad.

At that time my grandparents were renting a house. They had one younger daughter still at home and had already taken in another daughter with her two children. When my mother and I moved in, it made a total of eight people living in that old rent house. But, since it was fairly large, we had a bedroom all to ourselves.

Grandfather worked at Pennsylvania Iron Works in Beaumont as a night watchman for twelve dollars a week. Grandmother "took in" washing and ironing, and for a very small amount of money, once a week, she cleaned the building of the Assembly of God church which I attended with them.

My mother worked at the restaurant across the street from the courthouse in Beaumont. She earned five dollars a week. My aunt was a custodian at the courthouse earning six dollars a week cleaning and mopping floors. The mops were big and the water buckets were heavy. This later caused my aunt to have severe back problems. There was no workman's compensation or welfare to claim in those days, so she became one more mouth to feed—one more life to support. But without government help and with prayer and faith in God, all bills were paid and there was always something to eat.

While my mother worked at the restaurant, my grandmother took care of me. If she wasn't doing her own housework, she was always at the church, either cleaning the buildings or attending prayer meeting.

The place where my mother worked was just a few blocks from the port of Beaumont where ships came in to load cargo. One day, a certain seaman came into the restaurant and caught my mother's attention.

They had a few visits while his ship was still in dock, and she invited him to come and meet her parents and me. After he had made several more trips back to sea, they were married.

That was in 1937; I was seven years old.

Because my stepfather's Lykes Brothers ship docked more often at Houston than at Beaumont, he moved us to Houston. The small apartment he rented for us was only a few blocks from Main Street, right in downtown Houston. He continued to sail on ships because jobs were so hard to come by. My mother continued working at a restaurant.

When I got out of school each day I would go hang out with some older boys at the Penny Arcade, watching people play games.

Next door to the arcade was the Uptown Theater. You could see a show for nine cents, but I didn't have nine cents. One day, when I was standing in front of the movie house, two boys, about twelve or fourteen years old, walked up to me. Each was carrying a wooden box.

They said these were "shine boxes" and they made

money shining shoes. That sounded good to me. Even though I was only seven years old, I found a wooden apple box by a grocery store and made my own shine box.

With a can of black and a can of brown polish, a rag and a brush, I went into business for myself on Main Street.

A few days later, I found out I could join the news boys club and sell newspapers. I could make a half cent for every paper I sold and five cents for a shoe shine. The only problem was that not many people were buying papers or getting their shoes shined.

One very cold day I was shining shoes and I didn't have on any shoes. A very well-dressed man came up to me and told me he wanted to buy me some shoes. At least three times he begged me to let him take me and get some shoes. But, I lied to him and told him I had plenty of shoes at home, that I just liked to go barefooted.

So he just walked away.

If you found a good place to shine shoes, the older boys—who were mostly black, some Hispanic—would chase you away to take that place for themselves. Sometimes they would even beat you up.

I was much too little to fight them so I learned how to curse. I thought the louder and meaner I talked to them, the more they would leave me alone. But, instead I just developed a filthy mouth.

At the end of the year 1938, my step dad got a job painting houses and stopped going to sea. Most of his jobs were in River Oaks where the very rich folks of Houston lived.

During the summer when I was ten years old, my step dad took me to work with him; I scraped wallpaper off walls and applied the paste, while he hung wallpaper and painted the houses.

I continued working for him and by age fourteen, I was a journeyman painter. My step dad's rule was: if you ate at his table, you had to earn your keep. He was a hard man to work for, but this training from him helped me later to hold onto good jobs.

At the end of 1940 when I was eleven, we moved into a one-room house we had built fifteen miles from town. We had no electricity or running water. We cooked our meals on a little grill outside until we could buy a wood stove.

Early one Sunday morning, one of my stepfather's friends drove out to our place in the country to go rabbit hunting with us. When the hunt was over and we came back to the house, the friend wanted to show us his car. It was a second-hand Buick. What he really wanted us to see—and hear—was the radio in it.

He turned it on and the first words we heard was news that Pearl Harbor had been bombed. The men hollered at the same time, "We're at war!" I didn't know what war meant. I was only twelve years old at that time.

Things began to change very quickly. Gas was rationed, as was sugar and meat and coffee, as well as many other things.

Just a few months later, my Dad went off to work at a shipyard. He took our Model A Ford, our only car. My mother and I were left alone in the country for weeks at a time.

I had to walk seven miles to the nearest store when we had enough money to buy groceries. We had a cow and some chickens. Sometimes I worked in the peanut fields for fifty cents a day. Thank God I had a spirit-filled mother who prayed us through the hard times.

One Sunday morning I walked eight miles over to the home of a friend. We were going hunting. Someone in the family had bought an old shotgun for five dollars. It now belonged to my friend's fourteen-year-old brother, who had no business with a gun.

After examining the gun, my friend and I went to get a drink of water from the bucket and dipper that were on the porch at the back of the house.

While we were gone, my friend's brother loaded the gun and laid it across a chair. We came back to where the gun was, planning to go down to the creek to hunt rabbits. That's when, as I stated earlier, the boy stuck the barrel in my stomach, and laughingly, said, "We don't have to go hunting; I'm just going to shoot Bill."

Upon hearing the blast, an old man who had been sleeping in the house jumped up and started screaming as he ran out to see what was happening; we all took off running.

A few days after this incident, my friend's brother blew off the end of his hand; two weeks later another tragedy occurred involving that gun and the owner's older brother, Billy Kirk.

Billy and another boy were duck hunting. As they were creeping up through sparse weeds on a very low pond, the ducks flew off. Billy was in front of the boy who was carrying the old gun.

When they both rose up to shoot, the boy's finger slipped off the hammer. The blast caught Billy in his back and he died there in the pasture. The family finally realized how dangerous the old gun was and got rid of it.

When I was a little older, I met some kids at school whose father was the herdsman at the F&M Jersey Ranch. This man also trained horses and I liked horses.

I started hanging out at the ranch and learning a few things about horses. The kids and I would catch calves and put them in the pen so we could ride them later.

Soon I was going to youth rodeos and taking part in both bull and horse riding. During this time, my friend, Mr. Keen, the herdsman at the ranch, was helping me learn about rodeoing and teaching me how to train horses.

I enjoyed growing up in the country, especially working with the horses. It was surely better for me than the streets of Houston, and I was rubbing elbows with a better class of boys.

A Very Young Merchant Mariner

…but a foolish son is the heaviness of his mother
Proverbs 10:1

World War II was finally over on September 2, 1945. I was fifteen.

In December of 1945, my step dad told me he had heard that the Merchant Marine needed seamen. Since the war was over, many seamen had opted to stay home, leaving jobs for new men.

I decided to see if I could hire on as a seaman. I told my mother I was going to leave home and try to get a job on a ship. I knew this would break her heart, but I knew also it was time for me to get out on my own. So, with a few shirts and pairs of pants packed in a little bag, I started the twenty-mile hike to Houston and the National Maritime Union.

I finally reached the place only to find a long line ahead of me. I didn't know what to do, so I got in line.

There was a young man, who appeared to be about

twenty years old, in front of me. When he reached the man in charge, the man asked if he had any experience. He answered that he had been working on a tugboat. The man handed him papers to get a physical.

Then it was my turn. I stepped up. The man asked me if I had any experience. I replied, "Yes, sir. I've been working on tugboats." I'm sure he knew I was lying. But he asked me about my schooling, how far I'd gone. I told him, "Sixth grade." Then he gave me papers and told me where to go to get my physical.

When I got to the doctor who was to examine me, he told me to step on the scale. I remember hearing him say, "Boy, you're five pounds underweight. You're supposed to weigh at least 110 pounds."

Dejected, I stood there looking at him, and then he said, "I may not be doing the right thing, but I'm going to add five more pounds so you can pass."

Next, I was sent over to the U.S. Coast Guard to get my seaman's papers. They told me I would be an ordinary seaman and mess hall man. They said that meant I could work in the kitchen or mess hall or even on the deck.

I now had my papers, but I had to go back to the union hall to actually get a job. It was late when I got there and they seemed surprised I had passed the physical and received my papers.

After some time, the man in charge said. "All we have for a mess hall man is an old tanker at Corpus Christi that leaves for Bayonne, New Jersey, in two days."

They gave me five dollars to catch a Greyhound bus to Corpus Christi. Knowing I had two days, I put the money in my pocket and walked out to the highway and thumbed my way to Corpus.

When I arrived at the dock where the old tanker S.S.

W.W. Bruce was docked, I boarded her. I had little idea of what I was in for. I thought I had seen some characters on the streets of Houston, but these guys were rough.

A sailor came and took us to the cabin where we would stay. Then, I was taken to the galley where I was to work.

There was plenty to do. When I finished helping in the kitchen, I had to go to the mess hall to serve thirty-two crewmen their breakfast, lunch, and dinner.

After each meal I had to wash all the dishes and clean the mess hall.

We set sail for New Jersey the second day after I came aboard. The first five or six days at sea were good sailing.

In our "off" hours there was a lot of drinking and gambling on ship, in addition to swearing, cussing, and all kinds of profanity. I could swear and drink with the best of them, but I wasn't very good at gambling.

When we neared the Carolinas, approaching Cape Hatteras, the storm clouds grew very heavy and the waves began to pour over the deck of the ship.

As we went further into the storm, the ship began to "buck." The whole bow would go under, then the stern would come up out of the water, and the ship would vibrate because the propeller was out of the water. After that, the bow would go under again and when it came up there would be a wall of water coming down to midship. This was called "bucking."

For three days I was so seasick I was unable to work. The fourth day I was still sick but had nothing left to throw up.

I was out of my head. I went out of the galley on the stern of the ship and climbed upon the second rail of the deck. The third cook noticed that the big iron door, through which I'd come, was open and when he came to shut it, he saw me on top of the rail. He ran and pulled me off just before the stern of the ship went under the next big wave.

The same sailors who had been cursing and drinking and gambling when we had smooth sailing now began to sing the good old gospel songs I'd heard in church with my grandparents. Those men were scared. Later I found out that the reason they were so frightened was because the Cape Hatteras area was the graveyard for a great number of ships.

When we finally got to Bayonne, New Jersey, and the ship docked, almost everyone went ashore. A few blocks from the dock were the bars where there were prostitutes, pimps, and con artists.

I thought downtown Houston was bad, but it couldn't compare with New Jersey or New York. Although the snow was seven or eight inches deep, it didn't slow down our bar hopping and drinking.

Every night we were in New York, we took time to go to all the places of interest. Times Square was one of the greatest. It was my favorite place to party and drink. It had many bars, a lot of people, and a lot of activity going on. For someone who had never been in that big city, it was quite a thrill.

Even though I was only sixteen, I had no problem getting all the booze I wanted to drink.

After the ship had undergone two weeks of inspection, we were told it would need major repairs that would take a great deal of time. The crew was paid and then laid off to go wherever we wanted.

I went to Grand Central Station and bought a ticket to Houston. It was far from a pleasant trip. There was no air conditioning in the railroad cars and the windows were kept open. The soot from the smoke stack came in and settled on everything, turning it all gray.

It took a number of days to reach Houston. When we finally arrived, I took a bus and rode out to the city limits. Then I hitchhiked the rest of the way home.

My mother was surprised to see me, but very glad I had made it back home. She reminded me, "I have been putting the blood of Jesus on you every day that you have been gone."

I thanked her for her prayers. I didn't tell her that I almost got washed overboard. I didn't want her worrying when I went on another trip.

That came about a month later. I got on a ship, loaded with wheat, going to Japan, to the city of Yokohama. A few days after we'd passed through the Panama Canal, the refrigeration, which kept all our food supplies, went out. So, we had to head to San Pedro, California, for repairs.

We were told we'd probably be there about a week.

A few days later, a man came on board and said he had room for four men if they wanted a ride back to Houston. Four of us said, "We'll take it!"

We signed off the ship and headed home again.

It dawned on me that my mother and God must be up to something, because, once again, my trip had been blocked and I was well on my way back home.

One day, not long after I returned to Houston, I was visiting a friend at the same house where I almost got shot.

We were in the front yard. A man pulled up into the driveway and asked if we'd be interested in going to a little town south of San Antonio to apply gunnite to some oil storage tanks for Humble Oil Company.

I ran home to tell my mother I had a job and would be leaving early in the morning.

None of us knew this man, but my friend Joe and I, and another friend, were picked up at eight the next morning just as he had promised.

The three of us were still only sixteen, but the man thought we were eighteen. At any rate, we were off to a place somewhere south of San Antonio.

Hasty, Hasty Wedding

Look not thou upon the wine when it is red, when it
giveth his colour in the cup, when it moveth itself aright.
At the last it biteth like a serpent, and stingeth like an adder.
Proverbs 23:31, 32

The oil tanks we worked on were in Lytle, but we stayed in a little place called Natalia, where there was a motel and a bar and a little dance hall called Palm Courts. Many kids our age hung out there. It was easy to get drinks and dance and nobody bothered us.

Our boss, Mr. Shelton, hired a couple of local boys to work with us. One of the boys introduced me to his sister, Norma, who sold tickets at the local theater.

When that job in Lytle was finished, we moved on to Baytown to do more work for Humble Oil. On November 24, 1948, my friend Billy Ray and I took off a couple of days for Thanksgiving holidays. We decided to go back to the little town of Natalia to visit some of the kids we had met there and to do some partying at Palm Courts.

While we were sitting, drinking beer, the boy who had introduced me to his sister brought her over to our table. His name was Alvin.

He and his girlfriend and sister sat down and drank a few beers with us. Alvin and his girlfriend were only seventeen years old. His sister, Norma, was only sixteen and I had just turned nineteen.

We drank a few more beers.

Alvin asked me if I'd ever been to Bandera. I asked, "What's in Bandera?"

"It's a western town," he said, "like in the movies, with a lot of dance halls, with cowboys and cowgirls."

I borrowed Billy's car and we started for Bandera, about forty-five miles out in the Hill Country. We arrived there about nine o'clock that night.

It was just like Alvin had said—cowboys and cowgirls, a lot of drinking—even a few fights in the streets, and a lot of dance halls.

We were taking it all in.

About 10:30, Alvin and his girlfriend asked me if I would drive around and find a Justice of the Peace to marry them. We drove to a filling station and asked a black man who worked there if he knew a place where they could get married.

He said the only place he knew was in San Marcos. I really don't know how we got there, but about 1:30 a.m. we found San Marcos. We found an all-night filling station, and I pulled in to ask where to find a Justice of the Peace.

Again, the attendant was a black man. He gave us directions to where the J.P. lived. We found the place and Alvin and I walked up on the porch. It was a large house.

I knocked on the door, and a few minutes later light came on. An old man in his pajamas, and half asleep, opened the door with the expected question, "What do you want?"

"Are you the J. P.?" Alvin asked.

"Yes, I am," he said.

Alvin asked him, without hesitating, "Would you marry me and my girlfriend?"

He motioned for us to come in and then said, "I'll get my wife."

We all went into the living room. His wife came into the room wearing her nightgown.

Alvin asked, "How much do you charge?"

"For all four of you?" the J.P. inquired.

Quickly I said, "I ain't getting married. I don't hardly know this girl."

The old judge said, "Come on, I'll make you a real good deal—just five dollars apiece."

Well, we went for it and got married.

As we were signing papers, Alvin said, "Can you loan me five dollars? I don't have any money." So I paid the old man the ten dollars which left the whole sum of twelve dollars in my pocket.

We all trooped back to the old '41 Ford I had borrowed and started back to Natalia. I had to pick up my friend who had loaned me the car. We were supposed to be on the job at Humble Oil Company in Baytown at eight o'clock that morning.

When we got to Natalia about three o'clock, I pulled up to the Courts. "You three will have to get out here," I told them. "This is as far as I'm going."

I ran inside to wake up Billy Ray who was drunk. I got him into the car and called out to Alvin and our new wives, "Bye. I'll see you at Christmas."

As I pulled out of the driveway, I was burning rubber on the old '41 Ford. Only by the grace of God did my friend and I make it to Baytown in time for work that morning.

I didn't tell my mother about getting married. But a friend told his mother, and she told my mother. So, the secret was out. It was just a few days before Christmas, and we were all getting ready for a week of holidays.

My friend, Billy Ray, and I left Baytown and headed for Natalia. The highway from San Antonio to Laredo ran right through the little town.

It was about nine o'clock that night when we arrived. We stopped at Palm Courts. There was a party going on, but my wife wasn't there.

We hadn't communicated the whole month we'd been apart. I didn't have her address and she didn't have mine. I had never been to her house; I didn't even know where she lived.

I told my friend, Billy, "Well, she can't be hard to find in this little hick town. We've already stopped at the Courts. The only places left are the drug store and grocery store which are closed, the show, two filling stations, and three more beer joints."

We drove down the street and went into the Sunshine Tavern. The place was filled with people, and the jukebox was blaring out its country and western music.

There we saw Norma, sitting at a table with her mother and stepfather and her little sister.

The atmosphere was filled with cigarette smoke and loud noise. And through all of this, I was introduced to my new father- and mother-in-law who were already well on their way to being drunk.

We sat down with them and I bought several rounds

of drinks and a couple of packs of cigarettes for Norma and her mother. After the place closed, Norma's parents asked if Billy and I would drive them home. They had no car, so we agreed.

They directed us out of town to a dirt road with weeds about six feet tall on each side. About a half mile down this road, there appeared an opening in the weeds, just wide enough to drive the car through. Our headlights shone on the house.

This couldn't be the place, I thought.

But it was. The porch was about to fall in. There was cardboard in one of the windows, no electricity and no running water.

On the kitchen table sat a gallon of red wine and two bottles of whiskey. We all had a few more drinks and went to sleep.

Next morning when I got up, I was thirsty for a drink of water, but their bucket was empty.

"Where is your well?" I asked.

"There ain't any well," I was told. "Take the bucket and crawl through that barbed wire fence to the neighbors next door. We get water out of their cow trough."

When I got back with the water, we sat down at the table and had a few more drinks for our breakfast.

The next day, Billy Ray said he was going back to Houston to spend Christmas Day with his folks. I asked Norma if she would go back with us. Her answer was, "No." She wanted to stay and finish the twelfth grade.

I wasn't going to leave her, so I told my friend to go on back. "I'll come home after Christmas," I added.

As Billy drove away, I stood there thinking, *What am I doing? I don't even have a car down here and neither do these people.*

Settling Down Unsettled

Therefore shall a man leave his father and his mother, and shall cleave unto his wife: and they shall be one flesh.
Genesis 2:24

I got a job a few weeks later, working on a pipeline that was being built through the country. Not long after that my mother and Billy Ray drove to Natalia to see if I would come back to Houston.

This time Norma agreed to come with me, so we moved in with my parents. My step dad had added on to the little house, making it much larger. They had told us there would be plenty of room for us, and we agreed.

Also, my dad said he had several houses to paint in Houston—that I could come and help him. I took him up on the offer. And on weekends I rode in some local rodeos for the extra money. I still had the drinking problem and still loved to party.

At one of these rodeos my friend, Sam Keen, the horse trainer, asked me if I would like to come to work at the ranch and help him train horses. He indicated that he had more work than he could take care of and assured me that there was a house on the ranch that Norma and I could move into.

Furthermore, he said that he and his wife would help us get some furniture. When we agreed, they took us to a furniture store in Houston and helped us get credit so we could move to the ranch and into the house.

At the ranch, there was a nice big horse barn with stables and a large arena for training horses. Well-to-do people in the Houston area brought their horses here for training and also for boarding. My regular work day with the horses was about twelve to fourteen hours.

One day, three prominent men showed up at the arena. They were J. W. Lambert, who was constable for Precinct 2, Hugh Williams, who owned White Top Cab Company, and Mr. O'Neal, who was Superintendent for Houston Light and Power Company.

These men wanted to know if we could put a mounted constable drill team together to perform in rodeos and parades.

I took on the challenge and after several months of work with some thirty men and their horses, we had a team ready to perform in shows and rodeos in the Texas and Louisiana area.

When I was twenty years old, our first child was born. He was a boy and we named him Billy Sam.

At about this time Mr. O'Neal asked me if I would come to work for Houston Light and Power Company. He said they had a good retirement and insurance plan. The pay was also good.

He told me that his friend, Mr. William's, had bought

fifteen acres with a nice barn and stables and was in the process of building a big arena for rodeos. Since I was the drill captain, he said it would be nice if I would live on the place, rent-free.

I took the job with the light company and moved onto Mr. Williams place. Now we were closer in to Houston.

Everything seemed to be working out well. I even slowed down on my nightlife and drinking. In 1953, our second child, a girl, was born. We named her Brenda Ann.

Several years had passed since I had seen my mother and step dad. They called to tell me they had sold the place out in the country at Fairbanks and moved to the Heights in Houston and were hoping they could see more of us and the kids.

A few months later, we were working on a highline near my mother's house. I asked my foreman if I could run down a few blocks to see my mother. He said it would be all right, since it was about lunchtime.

When I knocked at her door she was really surprised to see me. She asked me to come in and she'd fix me something to eat.

Since my mother was always reading the Bible or praying, I didn't feel comfortable being around her very long at a time. I told her I didn't have time to stay and eat, but she pleaded with me.

"Let me tell you what I dreamed about you the other night."

"Mama," I said, "I don't have time to listen to what you dreamed. I've got to get back to the job to work."

But she insisted, saying it was from God.

"Okay," I consented, "tell me the dream."

She began, "I saw you standing behind the pulpit, preaching the gospel."

"Mama, you are crazy," I told her. "That will be the day." And I walked out the door and didn't even say good-bye to her.

My mother was a sweet and loving person, but because of the way I grew up, I didn't know how to receive or respect that love.

One day, Norma received a letter from her mother that brought her up-to-date on the changes in her mother's life. Her mother was no longer with the man we knew. The two had gotten into a big argument one night when they were out drinking and he left her, going back to his folks in New York.

So Norma's mother went to work in a beer joint to support herself and Norma's little sister.

About a month later, an old bachelor came into the place and they started dating. Three weeks later they got married.

It turned out the old man was one of the wealthiest ranchers in Medina County. He built them a new home and bought her a new car.

One day while I was at work at the power company, Mr. O'Neal gave me some nice cabinets to put in my garage. He told me to use the company pickup and take them on to my house.

When I pulled into our drive, my best friend's pickup was parked in front of the house. We had known each other since we were kids. I thought his wife was visiting my wife.

I unloaded the cabinets and went inside. I didn't see anyone so I went to the back porch. My little boy and girl were there eating cookies and drinking punch. They said they were having a party.

I went back into the house and into our bedroom. There I found Norma and my friend in the act of adultery.

My first thought was to kill them both.

I went for my gun in the closet.

As they begged for their lives, I chickened out. I couldn't pull the trigger.

My friend ran for his truck and sped away.

Norma confessed that this had been going on for several years.

It was getting late and I had to take the truck back to the substation and get my car. When I got back to the house, Norma began to beg me not to hurt her.

"You're not worth going to jail for," I told her. "I am taking you back to where I got you."

I felt ashamed. There were a lot of nice folks that we had been associated with and accumulated as friends over a period of time, and I didn't want them to know what had happened.

So, I quit the drill team and told Mr. O'Neal I was quitting my job. He couldn't understand why I would quit my good job, give up everything and move to San Antonio.

A few days later, we were loaded up and heading for Natalia. I stopped by and said goodbye to my mother.

"We're going back to Natalia," I told her. She knew something was wrong, but didn't ask any questions.

And so we drove away.

When we arrived at Natalia, we asked for directions to the Koenig ranch.

We found it a beautiful place with a nice home and a herd of white-faced cattle.

The next morning they took us further back into the ranch to the old farmhouse. It was old, but a nice home. They said we could have the house to live in.

When Norma had called her mother, Lucille, she only told her we were coming back to Natalia, but didn't tell her why.

After we unloaded our things into the house, Oscar, the old rancher who was now Norma's stepfather, wanted to show me around the place.

He said they couldn't irrigate from Lake Medina because things were so dry. Because of the drought he was buying hay from New Mexico and Oklahoma.

He said he had a Hispanic man helping a few days a week, but he was old and slow, too, like Oscar himself.

Oscar said he had never been married and had no sons and daughters to help with the cattle. He was already making plans for me as we rode over the place. He didn't know I was planning to leave Norma and go back to Houston and the Merchant Marine.

I just wanted to get away from everything and forget what had happened in our marriage. The only thing troubling me was the thought of leaving my little children to be raised without their real father.

I knew what it was like to grow up not having the love of a father—to have a step dad who didn't really love me.

After a few more days, I told Norma that I didn't love her, but if she was willing to try to work something out for the kids' sake, I was willing to stay for a while.

I told Oscar I'd help him in the evenings and weekends for the rent of the house. He said he wouldn't charge any rent; he was just glad to have some help.

That night Norma's brother, Alvin, and his wife came over. It was the first time we had seen each other since we left Natalia.

He related how he had been working at Kelly Air Force Base for a couple of years. The Department of Defense was just starting to build the giant hanger for the B-52 bombers. It was a big job.

He also said that work was beginning on Wilford Hall, the hospital for Lackland Air Force Base, and that Farnsworth and Chambers out of Houston was the general contractor.

The next morning I drove to Kelly Air Force Base. They said I couldn't come inside to the job site, but if I would wait at the gate, the project manager might come there to hire more workers.

I waited.

A little while later, a new white '54 Ford Sedan drove up and a small man got out. He was dressed in a white silk shirt with a little black bow tie and khaki riding pants and knee high riding boots.

I learned later his name was Jesse James.

Waiting for him with me were several large black guys and a few Hispanic men. I was the only white man there. I was dressed in a nice white shirt and blue jeans and black cowboy boots. It didn't look as if I was ready for construction work.

Jesse James called over five of the big black men. He gave them some papers and told them to go to Building 100 to clear in for passes to go to work.

He got back in the car and started to drive off. Then he stopped and rolled down the glass and said, "What do you do?"

I said," Anything, what do you need?"

He smiled and said, "Come, get in and go with me."

We drove inside the base. He asked if I knew how to use a cutting torch. I immediately said, "Yes, sir."

He pointed to piles of metal forms and said, "We have thirty-five acres of concrete to pour and all these forms have to have dowel holes cut in them."

He added, "We work twelve hours a day. We pay a dollar twenty-five an hour and you have thirty minutes for lunch. Be here at 5:30 in the morning."

Living Together;
Growing Apart

Such is the way of an adulterous woman; she eateth, and wipeth
her mouth, and saith I have done no wickedness.
Proverbs 30:20

When I arrived at Kelly Air Force Base at 5:30
the next morning, a truck picked us up at the
gate and drove us to the job site. It was mid-
summer and the temperature was between 95 and 100
degrees. Seldom were there clouds. (This drought was to
last nearly seven years.)

About a month and a half later, one of the foremen on
the project came over to where I was working and asked
me if I would like to work on the big crane as an oiler. He
said I would have to join the operating engineers local. The
pay scale was a dollar sixty-five an hour.

I took the job.

The next morning I went up to the crane. It was a 605
Koran (a big track crane with a 175-foot boom). I told the

operator I was as green as grass and had never even been on one of these things.

He said, "I know that, but Mr. James wants me to break you in. He said you were a good worker and he thought you might make a good operator."

After I had worked on the crane several months they moved my boss to another job and I became the operator of the 605 Koran.

One day when the workload was a little flat, I was singing some old country songs. One of the iron workers there had a country and western band.

He commented, "You have a good commercial voice."

He asked if I'd like to come by where they were playing and sing a little. I went by that night and sat in with the group of singers and musicians.

I sang a few old Hank Williams' songs and a few of Ray Price's and made a "pretty" good hit with the bunch.

Little did I know that this was to become more of a pitfall than anything else.

The name of the band was Jerry Dove and the String-busters. We generally played three nights a week in small, low class beer joints, but on Saturday nights we were booked into bigger and nicer places in and around the San Antonio area.

I was still running the crane at the big hangar. Occasionally, we moved the crane back and forth from Kelly to the Lackland Hospital. Our work day was still ten to eleven hours.

There was little to do at the ranch. Norma found a house at Natalia and wanted to move to town. The children were ready to start to school.

We talked with Oscar and Lucille and it was all right

with them—so we bought the house and moved in. The house was just a few blocks from the old Palm Courts.

A lot of young folks from Norma's school days still hung out there and Norma had more time to visit with them. I didn't like this, but since I was "doing my own thing," it didn't matter much.

After several more months the crane work was over and the crane was sent back to Houston. There was no other crane work available so I went to work for Gross Electric. They did contract work for Central Power and Light and also Medina Valley Electric Co-op.

The line foreman and I had been good friends before I went to work for Gross Electric. He was a heavy drinker and liked to party as much as I did.

I stayed with the band. We were even doing some recording at the T and T Studios in San Antonio.

Seven nights a week we spent partying or playing music somewhere. And, into this lifestyle was born our third child. We named him Joe Allen.

In the summer of 1956, my crew and I were working for Medina Valley Electric in Hondo. We were converting the town from 2,300 volts to 4,160 volts. This is called "hot line construction" which means you don't kill the voltage while working on the poles.

This is not the kind of work a man should be doing on Monday morning after drinking half the night before. But, we went to work in Hondo.

The foreman said we would complete the line work over Highway 90 and then make a decision on what else we would do, depending on the weather.

I climbed the pole and buckled my safety belt between the cross arm braces. I tied the hand line to the cross arm and called for the ground man to send up the rubber goods to cover the hot wires for safety.

I was also wearing my rubber gloves.

By this time we were all rather wet from the drizzly rain.

After I finished the work I sent the rubber goods back down. Then I realized the center phase should go on the other side of the kingpin for more clearance.

I climbed a little higher. I still had on my gloves. As I related earlier, I took the 4,160 volt line in my hand, lifted it over the kingpin and leaned back.

The back of my neck touched the bare 2,300 volt line. It sounded as if a large blast went off in my head. It was heard a block away.

The electricity went through my body and came out my left hip.

My foreman came up the pole to help me down. He was shaking like a leaf.

Although I was conscious, I couldn't move my arms or legs. I was totally helpless. I told him to connect my safety belt to the hand line, which would allow the ground men to let me down while he helped balance my body.

All the way to the ground I was using God's name in vain for my stupidity. Working in a state of being unable to reason, I had brought this on myself.

The hospital was only a few blocks away. The men loaded me into the pickup and drove me there.

After keeping me in the emergency room a while, the doctor transferred me to a private room. Although I couldn't move at all, I could hear.

I overheard one of the nurses asking the doctor, "Do you think he will make it?"

The doctor answered, "If his heart continues to beat,

he will probably be all right. We just don't know how much damage was done on the inside.

"Since the voltage came out the left side, he could develop heart failure. We will just have to wait and see. If he makes it through the day, he will probably be okay."

I don't remember anything from that moment until late in the afternoon. I must have slept all day.

When I awakened, I saw my clothes on a nearby chair. Weak and trembling, I managed to get them on.

I went out into the hall. There was no one there.

I made it to the front door and walked out. I barely managed to get down the short sidewalk to sit down on the curb.

It was not long before the foreman and one of the linemen drove up in the pickup. They helped me into the truck and we drove off. It was about five o'clock.

Six miles out of Hondo we came to a beer joint. Earl, my foreman, asked, "Do you feel like going in and having a few beers?"

I really didn't, but I said, "Okay."

My legs weren't working very well, but the two men helped me into the place and we sat at a table instead of at the bar.

I drank about three beers and then I told them, "I don't want any more. This stuff tastes like copper."

Earl said, "That's because the wire that burnt you was copper and now the copper from the wire is in your body."

We finally left the place two hours later and arrived at my home about nine o'clock that night. By then, I was even weaker, so my friends helped me in and put me to bed.

After a week of lying around the house doing nothing, I was fully recovered.

The Hondo job was finished and it would be two more weeks before the company began another. Work was slow everywhere. Only a few construction companies had cranes, and they all had their own operators.

Since I had nothing to lose, I decided to drive to San Antonio to see if the union had anything for me. The business agent said the only job available was at A. H. Beck Foundation Company. They just wanted an operator for one day.

No one else at the hall wanted a one-day job, so I drove over to the WOAI TV station where they were drilling the foundation for the big TV tower. As it turned out the job lasted three weeks.

Although I was not the drill operator on the crane, I was taking care of all the smaller equipment on the job. Mr. Beck liked my work, and when the job was over, he asked if I would stay on as a permanent employee.

I told him I would take it with full union pay.

He had taken a contract to drill all the foundations for the new North Star Mall Shopping Center and wanted me to be the drill operator on that job. His comment was, "It is a big job with lots of holes to drill. You will be there a long time."

Along with my decision to take the job I had another decision to make.

The main reason I had stayed married to Norma was to be a real dad to my kids, to see them grow up and to give them the things they needed. With the long drive each day from Natalia to North Star in San Antonio and back, eight to ten hours on the job, and still doing the music with the band at night, I had very little time with the kids.

The foundation company moved in on the job site a few days after I started the job.

Ruby is a Jewel

And whatsoever mine eyes desired I kept not from them,
I withheld not my heart from any joy…
Ecclesiastes 2:10

A crew of iron workers was brought in to tie the pylon steel that went down into the foundation holes and Jerry Dove, the leader of our band, was in that crew.

After work that evening, he told me that Mr. Tanner wanted us to come in Saturday to work on some new songs at the studio. He said we could use the studio all day and he would have his engineer run the recording equipment.

A few weeks later I was introduced to Leon Payne at the studio. He was a great composer of country and western songs. The biggest artists in that field of the entertainment business had recorded his songs—men like Hank Williams, Jim Reeves, Elvis Presley, and Ray Price, and many others.

We hit it off really well. I thought he was a tremendously gifted writer, and he liked my singing even though I was imitating other artists. He encouraged me to develop my own style and wrote some new material for me.

My relationship with Norma was going downhill; we were growing further and further apart. One night when I came home about ten o'clock, some of her friends were there.

We had a big argument. Even my oldest son was involved. I knew it was time to end our marriage so I walked out.

I left her and the kids, the home, a nice car that was paid for, money in the bank, and several credit cards. I left all my clothes—both work and dress. I left all my personal things that I had accumulated through our years together.

Leaving everything except what I was wearing, I drove off to San Antonio in my little Opal station wagon.

I rented a three dollar-a-night motel room on South Presa. It was an area filled with bars where drunks and prostitutes hung out.

I didn't like this environment at all, but it was cheap and also close to some of the joints in which our band sometimes played.

The construction business was booming and my company was staying busy. I was earning a good income which enabled me to send money to support my family.

I had hired a divorce lawyer, but for months he had been dragging his feet. He was taking my money, but doing nothing. I stayed too busy working and "night-lifing" to push the issue.

The company I worked for drilled the foundations for most of the hospitals on the medical hill on the north side of San Antonio.

One day we received orders to load the crane and all

of the equipment for a bridge job over the Cibolo Creek in the little town of La Vernia.

So we loaded up and moved to La Vernia.

We had the crane assembled and started to drill the foundation the day after we arrived. We had drilled down about forty feet when we hit solid rock—which meant we had about fifteen feet to go—and this was only the first hole.

The state engineer came over and stated, "Boys, it looks like this is going to be a long job."

It was already noon so I asked, "Do you know a good place to eat?"

"Yes," he said, "there are two restaurants in town, but most everybody eats at the Highway House. It's real clean and the food is like home cooking."

We took his advice and all went to the Highway House and found it just as he had said. It was very nice and clean. The waitresses were neatly dressed in white uniforms.

When we were seated at a table, a beautiful black-haired lady in white brought us menus and asked what we wanted to drink.

As she walked away from us, I looked at the engineer and asked, "Wow, who is that beautiful creature?"

He laughed and said, "That's Ruby. She's the owner, and, by the way, she's married."

We finished our meal and went back to work. We spent the rest of the evening and into the next day on that first hole.

The engineer was right; it was going to be a long job.

We continued to eat at the same restaurant.

Having to drill through rock, we worked long hours. But after work, the foreman and I would stop off at the restaurant to drink a few beers.

Ruby usually was not there in the late evenings. But the foreman, who had dated one of the waitresses several times, learned that Ruby and her husband were getting a divorce.

A few weeks after I heard about the divorce, Leon Payne and the band I was in were to play at a big dance at New Braunfels where Loretta Lynn was to be the featured singer.

I stopped at the restaurant to have a few beers. I shared with Ruby the news about the dance, informing her that I would be singing with Leon Payne and Loretta Lynn.

She laughed and said, "I would like to see that."

She then added, "You really know those people?"

I assured her I did and had even sung on the Grand Ole Opry show when it came to San Antonio.

She still didn't believe me. She asked me to sing a few songs for her, which I did. She was finally convinced and informed me that, if a waitress friend of hers would go along, she would go with me the next Saturday night.

When I arrived at the restaurant that Saturday, Ruby and her girlfriend were waiting, all dressed up in western clothes, boots and all.

Ruby had never seen me in anything but my work clothes, and I think she was pleasantly surprised to see me in my western duds.

When we arrived at the dance hall, we were invited to sit at Loretta's table. I introduced Ruby and her friend to Loretta and Leon and several other artists.

After the dance, Leon asked me if I would take him back home to San Antonio. The man who brought him had had too much to drink.

Since we had come in Ruby's car, I had to ask her if

we could take Leon back to San Antonio. Of course, her reply was positive.

Then she asked where I lived. I told her about Norma and our problems and about the motel room on South Presa.

She told me she had a vacant mobile home across from the restaurant, and inasmuch as I was working in La Vernia, and it would be better to have it occupied than left vacant, I could stay in it rent-free.

I moved in the next day.

In the few weeks I had been eating at Ruby's restaurant, I had noticed she was a kind and sharing person, even giving food and loaning money to those she knew would not pay her back.

She wanted to know if I was meeting the financial needs of my children. I assured her that they received a money order every week. When I showed her the receipts, her comment was, "I didn't think you were the kind to neglect the children."

It was not long before her divorce became final.

The job at the Cibolo Bridge was coming to an end. We were going to be moving to the Guadalupe River about twenty miles away to put in the bridge for Interstate 10. This was to be a bigger operation; everything had to be put on barges. It was going to be several months before the foundation would be finished.

Running Halfway 'Round the World

For all have sinned, and come short of the glory of God;
Romans 3:23

My relationship with Ruby grew stronger. We both felt we were made for each other. Although we still went out on Saturday nights, I was spending less time with my music and the band.

We spent more time at the restaurant in the evening, socializing with friends who came in for drinks at the bar area.

The only time Ruby drank was when we went to a dance and then she would have only a few mixed drinks. She liked dancing more than drinking.

Soon the job on the Guadalupe River was over. One of the guys on the crew we were working with reported that the Brown and Root Company was building big docks in Vietnam at Saigon and paying big money for experienced crane operators.

When I told Ruby about it, her only comment was, "I

thought you were going to settle down. But, if that's what you want to do, we can go check it out on Monday."

The restaurant was closed every Monday for cleaning and stocking supplies.

We drove to Houston on Monday to the Brown and Root office for an interview. Everything went smoothly until we discussed the pay.

I told the interviewer, "You must be crazy. I can make more than that in San Antonio with Beck Foundation Company."

His reply was, "But there are about three months you won't have to do anything because of the rainy monsoon season."

And I said, "Rain or no rain, I am not interested."

On the way back to San Antonio, Ruby told me the doctors had said she was not able to bear children. She said, "I always wanted a child, but after two marriages, I guess they were right."

I told her there were always plenty of kids without having any. She laughed and said, "I guess so."

We returned to La Vernia that evening and I went back to my job with Beck Foundation the next morning.

I finally had a talk with the lawyer who had been taking my money and doing nothing to get the divorce through.

He admitted that Norma was living with another man, but that she was not responding to the letters he had been sending.

It was then that I told him, "I'm hiring another lawyer and will not need you any more."

The new lawyer soon had things working in the right direction.

In November of 1965, after my Vietnam interview, an

old friend who was a project manager for Brown and Root in the Arabian Gulf told me about a job that would pay one hundred thousand dollars. I was interested.

A few days later, Ruby and I drove back down to Houston to Brown and Root headquarters.

I met with Miss Gloria Tumblin of the North Sea and the Arabian Gulf operation. Within a few minutes I had signed a contract for one hundred thousand dollars.

The company gave me a list of shots I had to take. After obtaining my passport that same day, we drove back to La Vernia. I would get my shots at the Nix Hospital in San Antonio.

I gave Mr. Beck a few days' notice that I would be leaving his company. He was somewhat upset but wished me well. He said Brown and Root had checked my records for supervisory ability and he had given them a good report.

Back in La Vernia, Ruby and I went to the bank and made arrangements for her to write checks from my account where the Brown and Root money would be deposited. She would also be sending money orders to support the kids every week.

That evening we started packing my suitcase for the trip.

Ruby looked at me with tears in her eyes and asked, "Will you be coming back?"

I told her, "I hope so. That place is halfway around the world, a lot of things can happen."

Then the tears came running down her cheeks as she said, "If you haven't noticed, I'm carrying your child.

"I went to the doctor, and he couldn't believe it. He had examined me before and told me there was no way I could have a child. He said, 'This is a miracle!'"

"Ruby, I'm sorry, but I have to take this job. Everything is ready for me to go."

"I understand," she said. "I'll be all right. Let's just stay in touch." And I promised I would.

The next morning after a few hugs and teary goodbyes, I drove off to Houston. I was going to ask my mother to drive me to the airport. I planned to leave my car at her house while I was in Arabia.

I hadn't talked or visited with my folks in several years, so they didn't know anything about my pending divorce from Norma, or about my relationship with Ruby.

My mother was, as always, glad to see me and wanted to know if everything was all right. I said it was and told her about the overseas job.

"I'd like you to drive me to the airport," I told them. "My plane leaves late this evening."

We had a good visit that evening. My step dad asked me, "Where in Arabia are you going?"

"Somewhere in the Arabian Gulf," I said. "That's all I know."

He said he'd been there several times on a tanker.

"It's very hot there," he said, warning me about the dangerous heat.

Then they drove me to the airport. My mother reminded me of the dream she had when I was twenty years old and how she always prayed and put the blood of Jesus over me.

I thanked them both and walked away to the terminal.

There I found ten other guys from Brown and Root in line; they were pipe fitters and welders. We boarded the plane.

When we were in the air, the stewardess asked what

we wanted to drink. We all ordered whiskey. She brought out a tray full of little bottles of bourbon. One guy even had his own bottle.

By the time we reached London, we were all drunk. The stewardess said, "There's no more whiskey—you guys have emptied the bar."

We all had a good laugh.

I remember that we had a four-hour layover. During this time, the police at the terminal kept a close eye on us until we boarded the next plane. There was no alcohol on this one and by the time we got to Cairo, Egypt, we were sober.

Here there was another two-hour layover. Finally, they let us board a plane to Bahrain. We arrived at eleven o'clock at night. There was no alcohol other than in the airport—and two bottles of beer was the limit.

I had finished one beer when a cabdriver came to take us to the hotel. The ten of us were loaded into two cabs for the drive.

The hotel was three-stories tall. The windows were open; there was no air conditioning. It was very hot—it must have been over 100 degrees that night.

About 5:30 the next morning I got up and went in the bathroom to shave. I looked in the mirror and something just hit me:

You're running. But, you are running from yourself. There is no problem back in America. The problem is looking at you in the mirror.

I didn't know where all that came from. It was a sobering thought that I had been running and running all through life looking for fulfillment. It was just fun and games.

I finished shaving and dressed. One of the other men and I went downstairs.

We looked into the mess hall. The food didn't look very good, and there were flies every where.

So we started walking the streets. A bunch of kids followed us, begging for money. There were even some people lying on straw mats on the sidewalks.

It looked as if there was an abundance of poverty—but, on the other hand, there were plenty of well-dressed people on the streets also.

We went to a bank to change some of our money so we would be able to buy something in Bahrain. We had time to kill because we had to wait overnight for the little two-engine plane that would take us over to Dyess Island where the construction of the operation would take place.

We walked around and found a little store that had American canned goods—Libby's Beanie Weenies. I bought a couple of cans, opened them right there, and ate my breakfast out of the can. I figured it had to be okay since it came from America.

After that, we walked around awhile to see the sights. Bahrain was a beautiful place overlooking the water. It was like Galveston, Texas. It was on the water and it was a resort.

There were people from different parts of the world. Many of them were from India. Most all the women we saw were dressed in black and had their faces covered—all but their eyes. I thought, *Man, they've got to be burning up in that garb.*

Down by a warehouse on the waterfront there was an old woman and four kids. Men from the warehouse were bringing out rotten bananas and dumping them into the water.

The kids jumped into the water and got the bananas. A man in the warehouse saw what they were doing and chased them away.

But, in a little while, they came back. They would retrieve the rotten bananas from the water and give them to the old woman. She was wearing something similar to an apron and she put the bananas in her dress and wobbled off down the street, holding the bananas with both hands. We didn't see her again.

Out in the bay was anchored a large, beautiful white yacht. We were told that it belonged to a sheik in Bahrain and had not moved from that place in six months. It had a full-time crew that traveled back and forth to shore.

The next morning the little plane took us to Dyess Island.

Too Far—Too Hot

…But where sin abounded, grace did much more abound:
Romans 5:20

B
ritish Petroleum had set up their headquarters on this tiny island. It was approximately a mile and a half long and a mile and a half wide. Our company had contracted with them to lay the offshore pipeline. It was a very large operation.

There were big lay barges, a huge sea-going type barge, as well as other barges. There were several large tugboats and a number of cranes.

There were also large stacks of pipe. This thirty-inch pipe had been coated with gunnite (concrete, so to speak) so that when it was laid and welded together, it wouldn't float back up. The weight of the concrete would hold it down until they began to put oil in it for the risers.

The reason this was being done was to accommodate the super tankers that came in from all over the world to pick up oil but could not come in closer because of the abundance of coral reefs. These tankers floated deep in the water and it was feared the coral would puncture the bottoms of the vessels. Risers were being built out in the

Gulf so that ships could be loaded out there. It was a large operation and a very expensive one.

For many years Brown and Root had been there off and on doing this work for British Petroleum. The Arabs themselves had nothing to do with the operation except to receive the money.

A large warehouse was located there. We were curious to know what was in it. We knew it was full of bales, but didn't know what was in the bales. We asked one of the guys who spoke English, "What was in the warehouse?"

His answer was, "The old sheik doesn't trust banks, so he took his money and baled it like hay or paper and stored it in the warehouse.

"But ants and rats and other rodents got in there and ate a lot of it. Now he doesn't know what to do."

This guy said that another company from England was coming to try to proof it against the rodents and ants.

The temperature on the island was about 120 to 125 degrees in the daytime with 100 percent humidity. It cooled off very little at night.

We slept in air-conditioned cabins the company had set up. The company also flew whiskey in for us because alcohol could not be bought there—and that was the only way welders and some of the others could be kept happy and on the job. A lot of drinking went on at night in the mess hall. The morning after our arrival we started to load pipe. We worked twenty-six hours straight, stopping only to eat. The company was way behind schedule on loading barges and laying pipe.

The lay barge was the L. E. Miner, and it was a huge operation in itself. Running up and down on it were large cranes which loaded the deck. It had twelve weld stations where the pipe would come in on big rollers.

The welders, called spark idiots, worked in air-conditioned tents. They also wore air-conditioned vests. This was the only way they were able to work twelve hours a day in that heat.

As sections of pipe were welded, they were moved onto conveyors and elevators lowered them down into the water. The barge moved very slowly laying the pipe as it was welded.

I had never seen an operation like this. It was tremendous and very exciting to me. I enjoyed it very much because there was never a dull moment.

We were waiting for a crane which was to come in from Houston on a Dutch freighter. It finally arrived several weeks later, but the freighter couldn't come in to the dock on the island.

We went out to it and spent all day getting the large crane out of the hold of the freighter and loading it onto a barge.

When we brought it back to the island, ten Arabs were assigned to help put the crane together.

This was quite an undertaking. Not one of them spoke English or knew anything about this giant Northwest crane.

Naturally, there was a lot of pointing and hollering and shouting.

I had to keep a cool head about me because these guys had little sense of humor. But, after working with them for a while, we became good friends.

One in the bunch had been working for an Italian engineer and had picked up a little Italian. When I used the little bit of Spanish I knew, it was funny that he could understand me. So between my little bit of Spanish and his little bit of Italian, we assembled the crane.

The only religious thing I ever saw over there were these Arabs bowing down to the ground and praying to their god, Allah. Five times a day—it made no difference what they were doing—the Arabs stopped what they were doing and prayed.

They had told us when we disembarked the plane in Bahrain, that if we had any Christian literature or Bibles, or anything religious, it was to stay on the plane. We were not to bring it onto Arabian soil.

I didn't understand at the time because I was not a Christian, I was not serving God.

But, there were a few guys on the job that were Christians. They made sure they didn't say anything about the Lord Jesus Christ while they were working on the island.

Now the operation was well under construction. Our regular work day was about sixteen hours. If we worked any longer—such as overtime, our work day would go up to twenty hours. That does not leave much time for rest and sleep.

Now I understood why the contract for each individual was so large; the contractors were getting their money's worth.

There was a man named Harry, an American, who had several tugboats leased to Brown and Root. He was pulling the barges for them.

One day when I was out on the barge in the 120 degree heat, the tugboat pulled up alongside.

Harry had ship-to-shore radio. He told me I needed

to go to the island—there was a phone call for me. I had no idea what the phone call might be, but I boarded the tugboat, and we went all the way back to the island headquarters where there was a phone.

I went into the radio shack and asked about the phone call. They said, "Yes, there is a number here and the operator will have to put you through to the States."

So they called from the island to Bahrain and from Bahrain to London and from London to New York and from New York to Houston and a little lady came on the telephone. It was my mother.

I couldn't believe what I heard her say, "Bill, isn't it hot over there in Arabia? I'm burning some leaves and trash out here and it's awful hot in Houston."

My answer was, "Mama, do you realize how much it took to get me over here for this phone call? Is that all you've got to ask?" And I hung up on my mother.

About that time the project manager, Johnny Clawson, walked in and asked me if there was an emergency.

Suddenly a lie popped into my head. I said, "Yeah, Johnny. That was my aunt calling. She said that my mother is in very bad shape and that I needed to go home to Houston."

I was surprised to hear him say, "Well, I'll tell you what I'll do. I'll get you a round trip ticket from Bahrain to Houston, because it will be cheaper than flying from here.

"Go take care of your business and then come back. I'll tell the pilot that he can fly you to Bahrain. Anyway, we need a few supplies."

So that evening I flew on a small plane to Bahrain. There I boarded a large plane, headed for the States.

The Hitchhiker That Saved Me From Judgment

That if thou shalt confess with thy mouth the Lord Jesus, and shalt believe in thine heart that God hath raised him from the dead, thou shalt be saved. For with the heart man believeth unto righteousness; and with the mouth confession is made unto salvation.
Romans 10:9, 10

The plane made several stops—London, Canada, and so on—and finally I arrived in Houston on June 9, 1966. It was ten o'clock at night. I located a phone and called my mother.

"Where are you?" she asked.

"I'm here at the airport in Houston."

She thought I was kidding her and said, "You're at the airport?"

"Yes," I told her, "I need a ride; would you come get me?"

So while I waited for my mother to pick me up, I called Ruby. She, too, asked, "Where are you?"

I told her I was in Arabia.

"No, I don't believe you," she said. "You sound real close. Where are you?"

So I told her I was in Houston and asked her what she was doing?

Anxiously, she said "My mother is about to take me to the hospital to have our child. We're going to the hospital in Seguin."

I assured her that I would be there as soon as I could make it.

When I arrived at the hospital, it was up into the day. Ruby had been in labor since ten o'clock the evening before and the doctors had done nothing.

I summoned the doctor and said, "You'll have to do something or I'll take her to San Antonio."

Finally, the doctors got their heads together and realized Ruby was going to require a C-section. They proceeded and the infant was delivered.

As I walked into her hospital room, the doctor told me, "It looks like you got here just in time to save two lives. We were having a problem, but everything is going to be all right."

Three or four days later they released Ruby and our son, William Charles.

In early September, 1966, Ruby announced, "I'm going to my Lutheran church this Sunday. I was reinstated while you were over in Arabia and you need to go with me."

I briskly replied, "No, I don't need a church. I'm doing all right the way I am."

"Well, the only way we are going to make it," she said, "is that we get into a church and get our lives together."

I had been drinking in the evenings with some of the members of the church, and they seemed to be pretty good guys—a lot better class than the iron workers I drank with before. So I agreed to try it.

On Sunday I went to church with her. The whole service lasted about an hour. After attending two more Sundays, I was asked if I would like to be confirmed. I agreed.

Then after I left the building, I asked Ruby, "What do they mean 'being confirmed'?"

"Oh, you have to go through some classes," she said, "and then they'll make you a member of the church."

Ruby liked to go to church because it lasted an hour, and then we could return to the café for the dinner run.

So this routine continued. I attended confirmation class for about six weeks and became a member of the Lutheran church.

My divorce from Norma was final on November 11, 1966.

Ruby and I were married on November 12, 1966, in the Lutheran church in La Vernia.

Hemisfair, a World's Fair that was to be held in San Antonio in 1968, was just coming up out of the ground. There was a large amount of construction going on. I went to the union and let them know I was back and to see if they had anything for me.

They had an immediate requirement for several crane operators to build the Tower of the Americas which would be the landmark of the fair (and San Antonio). They were beginning to drill the foundation and there would be an opening, so I was hired and helped drill some of the foundation for the Tower of the Americas.

Subsequent to that a crew from Ft. Worth, Texas, employed me as the crane operator to put the top house for the tower together. We worked twelve hours every day.

Not long after I became a member of the Lutheran church, I was asked if I would consider being a councilman since we lived in town and had a business there. So I again agreed and was elected.

A councilman is like an elder or a deacon in other denominations.

So, there I was, serving on the board of the church. I was still drinking. I was still cursing and doing my thing. Nothing had changed in my life except I was drinking with a better class of people.

We closed the restaurant on Sunday evenings at nine o'clock. Then several of the people from the church would come. The women would sit at tables over on one side and the men on the other. Of course, we were setting the beer up because we had keg beer at that time and we were just having a party, the men talking and women doing their thing.

And so our life continued in the same old way.

I was still stopping off in the evenings after work and drinking with the guys at some beer joint on the way home. Things were beginning to be like it used to be—hanging out a little late at night. There was a lot of work to be done at the restaurant, and there was a lot of work we were doing on the job, but the drinking was taking away my time again.

And, although I was serving on the board of the Lutheran church, it hadn't changed my life. In fact, I was getting back with the same bunch of guys that I used to run with. The habit was taking over more and more.

Ruby was getting discouraged and very dissatisfied.

We had several arguments. It looked as if things were not going to get better unless something happened.

At about this time I had an opportunity to get my oldest son a job working for the contractor at Hemisfair. I had to pull a lot of strings to get him on, but nevertheless, at seventeen we signed papers and a minor's release and got him a job. Now, he was working at a good job and making good money through the union.

Ruby always closed on Mondays to do ordering and cleaning. She would often meet me after work at Richter's Icehouse. I would leave my pickup and we would go to McCreless Shopping Center. We would eat supper at Luby's, she would do her shopping, then we went back to Richter's Icehouse where many of our friends would be gathered.

We would sit and drink and play pool—sometimes until eleven thirty or twelve o'clock.

This was the pattern every Monday. We had no other "pass time" because the restaurant was open six days a week and there was work to be done.

When the Hemisfair job was over, work began on building the large barracks at Lackland Air Force Base. I went to work for G. W. Mitchell, running one of his cranes at the base.

One Monday morning in August 1970, after one of these late Sunday drinking parties, I got up and started my drive to work. On my way into San Antonio, my life began to be revealed in front of me. It was like watching a television program—from the time I was seven years old, running the streets of Houston, through all the things I had been doing—drinking, "night-lifing"—the whole sorry thing.

In just one moment of time, it seemed the whole span of my life was completely revealed before me. I didn't understand what was happening.

Tears came into my eyes. I had never been on a crying drunk; I either wanted to love, or fight, but never to cry. But this Monday morning on the way to work, I cried out, "God, if this is you, and you are the God you claim you are, if you can clean this filthy thing up, I'll serve you the rest of my life."

I didn't think any more about it. I arrived at the job site at Lackland and went to work.

On the running board of my crane was a five-gallon water can. We put ice water in it every morning, but the iron workers would also bring a quart of vodka or a quart of gin and ice it down in that water can.

That Monday I didn't touch it. I wasn't drinking, I wasn't cussin' the iron workers; I didn't lose my temper. That's the way it went all day.

And when I was standing on the ground at five o'clock that evening, locking the crane, it dawned on me that something had changed.

I was thinking about an iron worker who we called Preacher. He was always reading a little black book and wouldn't hang out where we were because we were always cursing and telling our jokes.

Just then Preacher walked by, so I hollered at him, "Hey Preacher, I've done something today that I've never done in my whole life that I can remember."

He asked, "What's that?"

"I've been here all day," I said. "I haven't touched that water can with the vodka and gin. I haven't gotten mad at the iron workers."

His reply was, "I noticed that; I thought you were sick."

"No," I told him, "I had an experience with Jesus this morning, and I think He straightened out my life once and for all."

Preacher laughed and said, "Praise the Lord," and walked away.

I climbed into my pickup and drove to Richter's as I always did on Monday evening. I was going to have a few beers before Ruby arrived. When I went into the bar, a new bartender was working. I tried three times to order a beer.

Finally, the bartender said, "What do you want, Mac?"

For some unknown reason, I said, "Aw, just give me a coke."

I took the coke and walked to the front door of the little convenience store just as Ruby drove up. She saw me holding the Coca Cola.

"Bill, are you sick?" she asked. "What are you doing drinking a soda water?"

I explained, "I went in after a beer and I came out with this crazy thing."

She moved over to the passenger side, I climbed into the car and we headed to McCreless. We ate and shopped; then we came back. We pulled up beside my pickup at Richter's Ice House.

I climbed out and opened the door to my pick-up.

I heard my wife asking, "What are you doing?"

"Aren't we going in?" she asked. "Some of the gang is in there."

I answered, "No, you go in if you want to, but I'm going home."

Her reply was, "Well, if you're going home, I'm going home, too."

That was the last time I ever stopped at Richter's. I was totally delivered. I was set free from my filthy mouth and the desire for alcohol—all in one prayer.

I finally knew there was a power higher than the devil's power that had held me in bondage all these forty years.

That was in 1970. I was forty years old and I was reborn. Praise the Lord Jesus Christ!

The rest of that week, whereas before it had taken me three to four hours to return home from work at Lackland Air Force Base, I was home in about forty-five minutes.

Ruby didn't know what was happening, and I couldn't explain it to her.

But on Sunday morning, I walked up to my pastor and told him, "Pastor, I don't know what happened to me Monday. But, I've been home every night this week. I haven't drunk a bottle of beer or said a curse word. I've heard that you could have a personal experience with Jesus Christ."

He looked at me kind of funny and said, "You can have no such thing. Jesus Christ is for everybody. He doesn't single out individuals."

I said, "Well, Pastor, in my case, he did, because it feels like 10,000 pounds have been lifted off my shoulders.

"I feel good. I know that I am in my right mind, and I know that something has changed my life."

God Blesses With Prosperity

...and prove me now herewith, saith the Lord of hosts, if I will not open you the windows of heaven, and pour you out a blessing, that there shall not be room enough to receive it.
Malachi 3:10

Ruby was having a difficult time trying to figure out what had happened to me. A complete change had taken place. I no longer used foul language; I was not drinking beer and all the music I had loved so much, I really didn't care about any more.

I began listening to the gospel on the way to work, and at work, the iron workers wanted to know what had happened to me.

I told them, "I don't know. All I did was pick up a hitchhiker on the way to work on Monday, and He changed my life."

They wanted to know who he was.

My reply was, "His name is Jesus." Then I told them

how God had brought me through a divorce, given me a beautiful wife, and given us a beautiful little boy.

I knew they didn't believe anything I told them, so I put a car radio with a loudspeaker into the crane, and they had to listen to the gospel preached all day long.

At first, they didn't like it, but I was in control of the radio. Then, one by one, ever so often, they would come to me to ask for prayer for a marriage that was failing, or a son or daughter who was on drugs or alcohol. Some even accepted Jesus as their Savior.

The Lord was not only blessing me spiritually, but also financially. One day a man who owned property on the highway was in the restaurant and Ruby asked if he might be interested in selling to us.

He said he hadn't thought about selling, but he might consider it.

A few days later he came back and said he would sell the ninety acres on the highway for forty thousand dollars with a small down payment. We took him up on the offer. In a few months I was able to sell forty of the acres. This enabled us to pay off our debt and still own fifty acres.

My step dad had suffered a stroke and had to quit his painting business, so I moved him and my mother out onto this new property. Then I moved my family there also.

My mother was standing on the front porch one afternoon and said, pointing to the corner of the property, "Wouldn't that be a good place for a prayer meetin'?"

I said, "Mama, there's nothing out there but a field."

"It was just a thought," she murmured as she went back inside the house.

The café business was doing very well, but we needed more room for parking and a larger building. Across the highway was a nice building that a friend of ours had put up for a lounge and offices for his oil business. Next to it was a vacant property that came up for sale for forty thousand dollars.

I was talking to my friend about it, commenting that those people must be crazy to ask that much money for that property. He asked me if I was looking for a piece of land, to which I replied, "We're needing a larger place for the restaurant."

To my surprise he said, "You know what? I'll sell you this whole place, land and building for thirty-nine thousand dollars—nothing down, just make payments."

That evening we signed the papers on the property, which included a newer building, a large parking lot, and acreage in back.

We moved our restaurant across the highway and turned the original restaurant into a convenience store.

Not long after this, the oil business picked up. A man who had been in the oil supply business in Luling came into the restaurant. He asked Ruby and me if we had thought about putting in an oil field supply company.

He said he thought it was a good idea since a lot of wells were being drilled around La Vernia. He said if we would put up the money, he and his wife would manage it for a percentage.

We checked things out and went into another business.

I was still running the crane for a large construction company in San Antonio. Ruby called me at work one day and said that a Mr. Henderson who was in the house-moving business had come in to eat lunch. He told Ruby that his company was going to be moving some nice three-bedroom apartments that were across from North Park Mall to make room for the San Antonio Savings and

Loan building and that I should go by and look at them when I got off work.

I drove over to take a look and went into the office where I met Mr. Von Scheele. I told him that I had come to look at the apartments.

"How many do you want?" he asked.

Without thinking, I said, "All of them."

He was surprised and said that he had sold all but five. He gave me the keys so that I could look at them. When I went inside I couldn't believe how nice they were.

They were three-bedroom apartments with thick carpets. The kitchen and bath had tiled floors.

When I went back to the office, Mr. Von Scheele asked for my phone number. He said he would work out a price on five—he had never sold that many to one person.

I gave him our number and left. That was on a Thursday. When I came home from work Friday evening, Ruby told me the man with the apartments had called and wanted ninety-eight thousand dollars and twenty percent down. We laughed and agreed we didn't need any more debt. We still owed money on the restaurant.

My mother had been visiting her sister in Beaumont and was coming in on the bus to Seguin the following day. When I was driving over to pick her up, the Lord told me to go to San Antonio to see Mr. Von Scheele about the apartments.

I tried to push this out of my mind, but the Lord told me again.

When I picked up my mother, I asked her if she felt like riding into San Antonio and she agreed. I told her I was going to look at some buildings. I asked her to agree with me that if it was God's will, He would let the deal go through.

When we arrived at the office, Mr. Von Scheele said, "Come in and have a seat. I've got all the paperwork done. Ninety-eight thousand dollars will do it and 20 percent down."

I said, "Sir, I appreciate your time, but I told God if He wanted me to have the apartments, He would make a way, and if not, I didn't need them anyhow."

Mr. Von Scheele was amused, "I have never heard anything like that." We both laughed.

I shook his hand and told him, "It was nice doing business with you." I opened the door to leave.

"Wait a minute," he said, picking up his pen and starting to write. He kept saying, "I don't know why I'm doing this."

Then he said, "I'm going to let you have all five of the apartments for twenty-five thousand dollars and give you fifteen thousand dollars to move them to La Vernia."

The phone rang. He answered it and said, "Yes, he's right here."

He handed me the phone. It was Ruby who said, "I thought you would be there. Have you made a deal?"

I told her I had.

"Well," she said, "Mr. Hinby said he would finance them for us under one note since we were going to put the apartments on the restaurant property."

Ruby and Mr. Hinby did not know that I had made a deal lowering the price from ninety-eight thousand dollars to twenty-five thousand dollars.

Psalm 37:4 says, "Delight thyself also in the Lord; and he shall give thee the desires of thy heart." Some of the people were asking me—and even Ruby, my wife, asked me—"How do you make these kinds of deals?"

I said, "It's all in the Bible."

"And it shall come to pass, if thou shalt hearken diligently unto the voice of the Lord thy God, to observe and to do all his commandments which I command thee this day, that the Lord thy God will set thee on high above all nations of the earth: And all these blessings shall come on thee, and overtake thee, if thou shalt hearken unto the voice of the Lord thy God" (Deut. 28:1–2).

The Flu I Couldn't Shake

For indeed he was sick nigh unto death: but God had mercy on him...
Philippians 2:27

I spent all the time I could reading the Word and trying to find out more about this man called Jesus.

Although I had become a confirmed member of the church, and was serving on the board, I hadn't heard that I could be born again—or anything about faith—or that we had authority and power over all the powers of the devil. I realized that was why the pastor didn't think I had had an experience with the Lord on the way to work that Monday morning.

On Sunday mornings the people from our church would drop the children off for Sunday School, and then they would come by the restaurant and drink coffee and visit until church started. I would sit with them and get in a discussion about the Bible. I didn't know a whole lot, but

I felt they hadn't been born again and they knew almost nothing about the Bible.

So, every Sunday morning we had our little Bible study for about forty minutes; then we would go to the church for the service. Even Ruby could go and get back in plenty of time before the dinner run—when all the churches let out.

I was still trying to get Ruby to be born again. I kept telling her that being baptized as an infant didn't save her—that she must be born again. But this made her angry and we always ended up in an argument. This had been going on for several years.

Now there were five churches in La Vernia and almost everyone attending those churches ate in our restaurant on Sunday. I became good friends with the Baptist pastor. Sometimes we would talk about the Bible and even go into the private dining room and pray.

One day I asked him if he would baptize me. He said, "Yes, all you have to do is become a member of my church."

I told him that I couldn't leave our Lutheran church because I was still waiting on Ruby to get saved. And if I left, it would cause a lot of problems.

I asked if we could go to our house and use the swimming pool for him to baptize me. He said if he did, he would be "turned out" as a pastor in the Baptist church because I was not a Baptist.

"We sure don't want that to happen," I said. So, we dropped the subject, but we remained good friends.

My mother was driving every Sunday to a spirit-filled church in San Antonio. She told me not to be too hard on Ruby—that prayer could do a lot more than talking. I reminded her that this had been going on for almost eight years.

She smiled and said, "How long did I wait for you?"

I remembered that my mother never preached to me, even when I was running the streets as a child; she just kept the blood of Jesus over me in her prayers.

In 1978, I was working on the site of a large power plant under construction fifty miles south of San Antonio. By the end of November, the weather had become cold and damp.

On a Tuesday morning, I told Ruby, "I feel like I'm coming down with the flu." I had a terrible headache and I was feverish and weak. "If I make it through Friday, I'm going in Saturday morning to get a shot of penicillin."

When I arrived home Friday evening, I took a couple of aspirin and went to bed. The next morning I wasn't any better.

Ruby said she had to go to the restaurant for a little while and that if I would wait, she'd drive me to the doctor in Seguin. My answer was, "I can't wait—I'll drive myself."

At the clinic, there were three doctors' offices. I opened the door of the first office.

The doctor was sitting behind his desk. He asked me to come in and said, "Sit down. What can I do for you?"

I answered, "I've come to get a shot of penicillin to get rid of this flu."

As he looked at me closely he said, "I don't think you have the flu; I think you have a malignancy in your upper body.

He continued, as he took a thick book from his bookshelf and opened it, "I have never seen one of these but I studied about this in medical school." He added, "The left side of your forehead is covered with sweat, but the right side is dry. The pupil in the eye is the size of a pinpoint and the eyelid is covering half of the eye—and you should be having severe headaches."

My reply was, "I have been having headaches all week, but I think it is my sinus."

He disagreed and proceeded to x-ray the sinus. He was right. The sinuses were all clear. Then he had another doctor look at me. This doctor agreed that Dr. Lee was right.

So Dr. Lee recommended I see a doctor in Oak Hills Medical Center in San Antonio, making me an appointment for Monday.

I drove home and told Ruby what the doctor had said. I told her I would call the company for which I was working so they could get another operator to take my place. Then I went to bed and stayed there until Monday morning.

We arrived at Oak Hills Medical Center, and after five hours of examination, the doctor told us everything looked good. So, we drove back home.

The next morning my head was still hurting and I didn't feel well, so I drove back to Seguin. This time I went to see an ophthalmologist, Dr. Fleming. I told him what Dr. Lee had said about my right eye and the headaches. He examined me and said, "You have Horner's syndrome. You do have a problem."

He told me he had attended medical school with a Dr. Bajandas, who was now teaching at Bexar County Teaching Hospital in San Antonio. "If anyone can find the problem, he can."

I agreed to let him make an appointment for me, so he called and was able to make arrangements for the next day.

When we arrived at the hospital, I was met by a team of doctors who worked with Dr. Bajandas. After several hours of x-rays, we met Dr. Bajandas.

He told us this type of tumor was very rare; that it was growing in the nerve duct behind the right eye and that it would be a very delicate operation because the nerves could be damaged when they removed the tumor.

He explained that the nerves connect with the brain and that damage to them could cause a severe problem for life, but the tumor would definitely have to be removed.

He continued, "I am going to give you some codeine tablets to take for the pain until we decide when we will operate. We will study the x-rays in detail and then we will let you know when to come in."

As we left the hospital, Ruby dejectedly said, "That sure wasn't a good report."

My response was, "Ruby, God is going to remove the tumor."

She said, "Are you crazy? You heard what the doctor said. It's one in a million. God doesn't remove tumors; that's why we have doctors."

When I got home I prayed, "God, you have got to help me." I picked up the Bible not knowing where to read. So, I just opened the Bible and Hebrews 13:8, "Jesus Christ the same yesterday, and today, and forever" rose up off the page. It seemed like it was in giant print.

I called for Ruby to come see the scripture. She looked at it and asked what it meant. I told her it meant that Jesus is still performing miracles.

Immediately she said, "That's not what it means. When Jesus went to heaven and all the disciples died, there were no more miracles."

"Who told you that?" I asked.

She answered, "Our pastor has always said it."

"That's why they never tell you to bring your Bible," I told her. "You believe what you want to believe, but I'm going to believe what the Bible says."

Ruby replied sharply, "You think you know more than the pastors," and walked out of the room.

I turned a few more pages and found 1 Peter 2:24, "Who his own self bare our sins in his own body on the tree, that we, being dead to sins, should live unto righteousness: by whose stripes ye were healed."

I had never seen these scriptures in the Bible, but I knew they were there for a reason.

I wasn't able to do any type of work because the pain kept getting worse. It even got so bad I didn't want to get out of bed. I still hadn't touched the codeine tablets the doctor had given me.

Several weeks passed, and we still hadn't heard from the doctor. Ruby was getting very upset and thought we should see another doctor.

I tried to convince her I still believed God would remove the tumor. I didn't know how He would, but I knew He would.

At two a.m. on a Wednesday morning, the pain was so bad I couldn't stand it. I got up and went into the bathroom. I took the codeine pills from the medicine cabinet and poured about half of them into my hand. Before I could put them to my mouth, out of my spirit it seemed as if the Lord said, *Are you trusting me or the pills?*

I put them all back into the little bottle and put the bottle back into the medicine cabinet.

When I laid my head on the pillow, Ruby asked, "How many did you take?"

I said, "None of them." And immediately I went sound asleep.

The next morning the little clock radio came on. Ruby left for work; our son Billy left for school. The house was empty.

There was a faint pain that came and went; I would drift in and out of sleep.

The radio was still playing. About 8:30 a preacher was closing his message. I didn't hear his message, but he said they would be having a prayer meeting at ten o'clock that morning, and if anyone had a need, they should come to the church. There they would pray the prayer of faith and God would meet their need.

An audible voice spoke in my outer ear and said, "*Get up and go.*" It seemed as if I drifted off to sleep, but a short time later, the voice came again.

I raised up on my elbows to see who was in the room, but the room was empty. The voice was the same—very deep—and it said, "*Get up and go.*"

So, I got out of bed, dressed, and drove to the restaurant. As I entered the office, Ruby looked at me and asked, "What are you doing out of bed?"

I told her I was going to a prayer meeting.

She replied, "Bill, we don't have prayer meetings at our church!"

"I know that," I said. "I'm not going to our church. The Lord told me to go to San Antonio. They're having a prayer meeting on Steves Street."

Ruby wanted me to sit down while she called the doctor. "You're having a seizure; that thing is getting to your brain."

Without hesitating, I said, "Call the doctor if you want to, but I'm going to San Antonio."

"Bill, I can't go with you," she said. "I've got a salesman coming this morning. How do you think you can make it to San Antonio in the shape you're in?"

I knew I had to do this, so I said, "I don't know, but don't worry. I'll be all right."

Doctors Confirm Healing

He sent his word, and healed them, and delivered them
from their destructions.
Psalm 107:20

As I drove toward San Antonio, it seemed that the
terrible pain that had caused me to get up earlier
that morning was returning with more intensity.

I drove on, not knowing exactly how far I had to go. (I
later learned that it was twenty-five miles to the church.)
I turned onto Steves Street and drove quite a distance. I
passed one church, drove a few more blocks and came to
another church. I felt as if this was the one to which the
Lord had told me to go.

I turned into the parking lot, parked my car, and
walked to the side door of the church. It was locked, so I
went to the front door. It was also locked.

The pain was now weighing me down; my head was
hurting so badly. I spoke out loud: "God," I said, "I am
going to give you one more chance. I know you told me

to come, for I heard you very clearly. But why is the door locked? There is no one here. I am going to drive around the block, and I am trusting when I get back, the door will be open."

I returned to my car and drove out of the parking lot. I drove down Steves Street and came to a street called South Presa, but there was no short block, so I had to drive two or three blocks before I could cut back through on Hackberry.

I came back down Steves Street and entered the parking lot of the church. As I drove in, I saw a man at the side door. He was unlocking the church.

I parked my car, walked over to him, and asked, "Are you the Pastor?"

He answered, "Yes, I am."

"I didn't come to join your church," I told him, "but I came to get something from God this morning."

His reply was, "Well, brother, these doors swing both ways. We don't have a membership here. You are welcome, come on in."

I went in and sat on the second pew. The pastor went about turning on the lights and air-conditioning.

In a few moments I heard people talking and saw a few old-fashioned looking grannies come in. Most of them wore their hair long and done up in a bun. One of them sat down at the piano, another came in with a violin, and still another was carrying an accordion.

They stepped up on the stage and began to tune up. I thought to myself, *What kind of show is this going to be?* I sat there in my pain and waited. There were about ten old women who came into that prayer meeting. They began to play their instruments and to sing some old familiar songs.

After several of these songs, they had a little testimony service, and one granny, who looked as if she might be eighty-five, stood up and patted her stomach. She said, "Twenty years ago, they were going to cut out my gallbladder, but I came to a prayer meetin' like this one and the Lord healed me—and I've still got that gallbladder. Glory be to God."

Then another one got up and gave her testimony. I thought, as I sat watching all of this, *Well, maybe this is the right place.*

They sang a few more songs. Then the pastor stood up and read some from the Word and expounded a little on what he had read. He spoke about ten minutes.

Then he added, "We have a brother with us this morning who needs a touch from God."

I hadn't told him that I had a tumor; I hadn't told him why I had come. I looked around to see who the "brother" was. I had been in a church regularly for nearly twelve years, even serving on the board of that church, but I was not familiar with the term "brother."

Now these people were calling me brother.

The pastor pointed to me and said, "Come up."

I went down toward the little pulpit. He wasn't on the main stage but was on the floor where he could teach this small group.

As I walked toward him, he reached behind his little pulpit and pulled out a bottle of oil. (I remembered when I was a boy, staying with my grandmother, she would give me a dose of castor oil, and then she would pray for me.) I thought, *I am not going to drink that oil.*

At that point, all the women got up out of their pews and started toward me. I thought they were going to try to hold me down and make me drink the oil. I didn't realize they were just doing what the Bible tells us to do in Mark 16:18, "…lay hands on the sick, and they shall recover."

The pastor put a little of the oil on his finger and then put it on my forehead. This was all foreign to me. I hadn't read far enough into the Word to know about James 5:14–15, "Is any sick among you? let him call for the elders of the church; and let them pray over him, anointing him with oil in the name of the Lord. And the prayer of faith shall save the sick, and the Lord shall raise him up…"

So, he anointed my head, and they laid their hands on me, and began to pray in that heavenly language. Instantly, the excruciating pain that had come over me on the way to San Antonio disappeared. I shook my head because it felt so good. There was no pain.

I thanked them and left the church building. I walked to the car and climbed in. I must have driven seventy miles an hour back to the café. I walked into the office and announced to Ruby, "I got my healing."

She looked at me, questioningly, and said, "I don't know where you've been or what you've been involved with, but while you were gone, Dr. Bajandas called. He wants you to come in tomorrow morning and let them run a few more tests and set you up for surgery."

My reply was, "I would be a fool to go in there the way I feel now and let them cut on my head. Ruby, there has not been one bit of pain since those people prayed for me. My eyes are focused, clear—and I feel good."

Then something seemed to just rise up in my spirit. It wasn't the audible voice I had heard that morning when He told me to get up and go to the prayer meeting; it was in my spirit.

It said, *Are you going to go so I can prove through medical science that I touched you and made you whole?*

I turned to Ruby and said, "Okay, we'll go in the morning."

We got up early because it would be a long drive to the hospital in San Antonio. Ruby wanted to drive, but I said, "No, I'm feeling fine. I'll drive since you are not used to driving through all the traffic."

Ruby was quietly weeping because of the bad report from the doctors. I was weeping, too—but my tears were tears of joy because I knew the tumor had been dissolved.

At the hospital Ruby had to stay in a large waiting room. I was taken into a long room attended by technicians that had monitors along the length of the room.

The technicians had me remove my clothes and put on a gown and took me to another room where there was a dome-shaped machine. It had a bed and they laid me on it and strapped me down.

Either the bed or the dome began to move until it covered half my body. I lay there a long time—for what seemed like hours. Finally, they took me out and I was sent to have more x-rays taken. I was told by the doctor that thirty or more pictures were taken.

Once again the attendants took me to another machine and strapped me to its bed. Again, the machine covered me, and, again, I was there several hours. When I finished I was sent for more x-rays.

At five thirty that evening, they dismissed me. I had been there with the technicians eight hours and I had not seen Dr. Bajandas.

As I walked down the hall to the waiting room, Ruby, who had been crying, stood up. "Oh, Bill," she whispered, "what in the world have they been doing all this time? I thought they were operating on you."

"No, Ruby," I told her. "They're still trying to find that

tumor that God took out of my head. I haven't seen the doctor—they won't tell me anything."

We sat down. I looked down the hall and saw Dr. Bajandas coming toward us. He had a big smile on his face. I nudged Ruby and told her, "Ruby, he has a good report; he's smiling."

He walked up to us and said, "Bill, I don't know what's happened. I have no explanation. I am teaching medicine in three hospitals. I have an excellent team of doctors. In our previous tests we found a tumor, but today, there is no tumor.

"If we had used only the one machine, I would have my doubts—but the scan machine (he called it a slicer) does not miss a thing. If there had been a tumor there, it would have shown up. But, there is no tumor in your head today."

As we left the hospital and were going down the steps, Ruby stopped me and, looking into my eyes, said, "They missed it."

"Woman!" I said, "Can't you believe anything? I told you that I feel like a million dollars. I told you that God took that thing away yesterday at that prayer meeting. The doctor even told you that there is no more tumor. What is it going to take to make a believer out of you?"

She laughed. We found the car and drove home.

That Friday and Saturday I went to the restaurant. I was feeling great and completed some work that I had been putting off.

I was sitting, drinking some iced tea, when people began to come in and were amazed to find me there. They thought we had gone in for the surgery.

They asked, "What did they do? We don't see any bandages. You're out of the hospital already?"

Ruby came over and began to tell them, "No, the doctors said the tumor is gone. There is no tumor."

They looked at us in a strange way; we could see the skepticism in their faces.

Sunday morning we got ready and went to church. I walked up to the pastor as he was putting on his robe, getting ready for the Sunday morning service.

I said, "Pastor, I have been serving on the board of this church for five years. I painted the steeple and covered the old abandoned well. I've done a lot of work around here. You know me very well.

"People from San Antonio to Victoria knew I was facing brain surgery, but I went to a prayer meeting Wednesday morning and God took the tumor away. It was verified by a team of doctors at Bexar County Teaching Hospital. They gave me a clean bill of health and said there was no longer a tumor in my head. I think I should go before this congregation and tell them what Jesus has done."

His reply was, "Bill, do you think I am going to let you go before my congregation and tell a story like that? Make a fool out of God? Make a fool out of yourself? And, especially make a fool out of me?"

I thought a minute and then told him, "That's all right, Pastor. They'll be down at the restaurant soon after you dismiss them, and I'll tell them there."

He went on with the service and preached his little "sermonette." We sat and listened. At the very end, when he was getting ready to dismiss the people, he stood up and smiled a little smile—even snickered a little bit—and said, "Mr. Moore has a story he wants to tell you."

Then he sat down behind one of the pulpits, as if to say

he didn't want to be a part of it. Nevertheless, he allowed me to come up.

I began to testify and I told the people what had happened.

When I arrived at the restaurant, many of the people from the church gathered around me. They wanted to know if what I related really happened—did I really have a tumor.

I told them, "Yes. It was verified that I had a tumor. Then I went to a prayer meeting on Wednesday morning, and a group of ladies and a pastor laid hands on me and anointed my head with oil…"

Those Lutheran people looked at me and said, "With what?"

"With oil," I repeated and went on with my story. "God removed the tumor. I spent eight and a half hours at Bexar County Teaching Hospital Thursday. It was proven over and over in their scans and x-rays that there is no tumor—no reason to operate."

People from the other churches in town came into the restaurant that Sunday and the days following wanting to know how the operation went, or when it was to be done.

We were able to tell them there would be no operation—that God had removed the tumor. They all had problems believing the story. Nevertheless, they had the fruits of it before their eyes.

It could not be denied that I was up and around, working, and living my usual life. It was simply a miracle of God!

No Longer Welcome

...Whether it be right in the sight of God to hearken unto you more than unto God, judge ye. For we cannot but speak the things which we have seen and heard.
Acts 4:19,20

In August of 1979, I was still going to our Lutheran church on Sunday morning, but on Wednesday night we didn't have services there, so I would drive to San Antonio to attend Alamo Revival Center.

The first couple of Wednesday nights, my son, Bill, wanted to go with me.

I resisted, "Bill, there are enough problems now with your mother without adding another. When you accept Jesus as your Lord and Savior and you know that you have, then you may go with me if you still want to."

He replied, "Dad, I did! Last night I knelt by my bed and I accepted Jesus Christ. You've been telling me about him, and I accepted him. I want you to come into my room," he told me.

"There are no more big Elvis Presley posters on my wall. I packed up all my tapes and I'm going to give them all to Joey. So why can't I go with you?"

I finally consented, "Okay, next Wednesday night I'll let you go with me."

Then I had to tell Ruby, "Little Bill wants to go with me next Wednesday night. It's just about two weeks before his confirmation. Do you think it will be all right?"

Angrily, she said, "I told you I didn't want to hear any more about your Jesus; I don't want to hear any more about Alamo Revival Center; I want you to leave me alone about this."

I responded, "Sorry. I'll not bring it up again."

So I went down to the hay barn to get away. For three consecutive days I went there to pray to the Lord, saying, "God, if it takes the farm, the businesses, and this family, I'm not going back to the place, the lifestyle that I came out of. God, You're going to have to do something."

The following Wednesday I went back to Alamo Revival in San Antonio. When services were over, I was told not to miss the next Wednesday, because a medical doctor from San Antonio was coming to speak—a Dr. Kenneth Burton. It was announced that he was a flight surgeon for General Eisenhower; that he had just returned with Pat Boone from Israel; and that he would be speaking on the "End Times."

I knew that we had not heard much—or anything at all—about the "End Times."

When I arrived home, I thought, *I'll try one more time.* I said to Ruby, "You need to go with me next Wednesday. Dr. Kenneth Burton is going to be speaking on the 'End Times.'"

She glared at me, "I told you I didn't want to hear any more about what goes on at those meetings. Now, either you get right, or I'm going to Floresville and I'll get a lawyer, and we'll end this relationship."

I replied, "Excuse me, ma'am. I promise you I won't mention it again."

She turned and walked away, but in a few minutes she came back. "What did you say that doctor's name was?" she asked.

"Kenneth Burton," I said.

"You know," she told me, "years ago we had a family doctor named Kenneth Burton. He was practicing in San Antonio when we lived there." She said, "I wonder if this is the same doctor."

I remarked, "No, this doctor is a Christian. That old doctor is probably dead by now, anyhow." This put an end to that little conversation.

But, when the following Wednesday came, and little Bill and I were getting ready to go, I walked down the hall and passed the bathroom door which was partially open. Ruby was at the mirror applying make-up to her face. She had put on a really nice dress and was obviously getting ready to go out.

I thought, *I wonder where she is going*. So, I just asked her, "Where do you think you're going tonight?"

She smiled at me and said, "Oh, I think I'll go with you and Bill tonight. I'm curious to see if that's the Dr. Burton that used to be our family doctor."

I thought, *Well, those three days in the hay barn must have paid off because God is melting her heart.*

The three of us got into the car and drove to San Antonio to the Alamo Revival Center. When we entered the parking lot, there was only one other car there—a big white Cadillac.

(I always tried to get there a little early.)

As I drove up to park beside the Cadillac, a gentleman

was getting out. "I am Dr. Kenneth Burton," he said. So I introduced myself, "I'm Bill Moore."

About that time, Ruby came around to our side of the car. Dr. Burton looked at her and said, "Ruby, what in the world are you doing here?"

She answered, "I don't know, Dr. Burton. God's been doing so much in Bill's life, I just thought I would come and check it out."

He gave her a big hug and they started walking across the parking lot toward the church building. Bill and I followed along behind them.

We heard her ask, "Dr. Burton, what kind of a church is this?"

He replied, "Oh, it's kind of like the Assemblies. They believe in the Gifts of the Holy Spirit; we believe in healing and we believe in miracles."

And, as they walked down the sidewalk, he told Ruby his story, "My wife and I were Baptists. One night I had a dream. In the dream I was in Detroit, Michigan, at a Cadillac factory. I was looking at a row of Cadillacs that were parked on a hill and those Cadillacs started rolling down the hill. But when they reached the next hill, they started rolling back. They couldn't climb the hill."

Dr. Burton continued to relate his dream. "I questioned why these Cadillacs didn't have power to climb the hill and a voice spoke out and said, *These are not complete. They have no engines.*

"When I woke up, I was speaking in a new language. It almost scared my wife to death. She didn't know what had happened, but God had filled me with the Holy Spirit."

By this time, Dr. Burton and Ruby had reached the side door of the church. We went in and sat down together.

As the people arrived before the service, they came over to shake Dr. Burton's hand.

He introduced them to Ruby—and they all hugged her.

Both men and women came and stood around us. They knew about the testimony of how God had, through a miracle, taken away my tumor. Everyone was so friendly.

Then the service began and we listened to Dr. Burton speak.

On the way home, it was easy to see that Ruby had been impressed with the people of the church.

"Wow! Man, those people down there love. I've been in church all my life and never got a hug." She paused, then said, "It seemed like every one in that place was hugging people. And there was a really friendly atmosphere."

I said, "That's what happens when you're born again. The old man has passed away and the new man has come alive in you."

She laughed and said, "Well, I think so, because it has surely changed you."

We returned to our church the following Sunday. After we arrived at the restaurant, Ruby told me, "You know, Bill, I don't think I can go back there again. That's the coldest place I've ever been. I didn't realize how cold it was."

"Well, Ruby," I answered, "evidently God has something better for us."

A few days later, we received a letter from the church stating that we were no longer worthy to worship in the Christian community and they were removing our membership.

Ruby shed some tears, but she knew that it must be God doing something in our lives.

Two weeks after my healing occurred, the union called. They had learned that I was well and wanted me for a job running a crane in Panna Maria, which was about twenty miles away. They said it would be light duty. They were digging for uranium at the Chevron plant.

That Monday as I drove down the highway toward Stockdale, I was reliving all the things the Lord had done for me—how He delivered me from alcohol addiction and the nightlife that went along with it—the sinful life I had lived so long. And, how He had now healed my body of a tumor and had given me such peace.

Suddenly, my hands lifted up off the steering wheel as I turned onto Highway 123 going to Panna Maria. I drove the whole stretch with my hands off the steering wheel until I reached the Chevron plant and turned onto the road that led to the construction site.

I didn't realize what was happening until I arrived at the job site and the wide road that led down to the plant. My hands came down and took hold of the steering wheel and I was speaking in a beautiful language.

I was unaware of the cars I passed or the bridges I crossed. I was not driving the truck.

I was literally praising the Lord and I knew that the Holy Spirit was real. I had heard about it. My mother and my relatives had it, but I hadn't known it was for me. But, I had found that it is for everyone as I began to read the Book of Acts.

Miracles in a Garage

...Surely the Lord is in this place...
Genesis 28:16

We didn't know where to go; we didn't know what to do.

People kept coming to our house on Saturday nights wanting to hear all about the miracle—wanting to know if Jesus still does those things. Some of the Lutherans said they'd been in church all their lives and had never heard anything like it.

But, they knew we couldn't be lying because we had the doctor's report to prove it.

So, we began to hold little "services" in our home. Finally, there were so many people coming that we didn't have room for all of them in our house.

Ruby bought thirty folding chairs and we set up for services in our garage. Since we drove to San Antonio on Sunday mornings to attend Alamo Revival Center, we changed our services from Saturday night to Sunday night.

So on Sunday evenings people would come to the garage where I preached to them and taught them about the healing power of Jesus. I only knew a few scriptures, and I was frightened because I didn't know enough about the Bible, and I still didn't want to be a preacher. I had to study more than ever, but the people kept coming and we didn't know what else to do with them.

Since we received the letter putting us out of the church, our son didn't get to go through confirmation. However, many of the church members didn't know about the letter and some of Ruby's relatives got upset with us for leaving the church and taking little Bill out before he was confirmed. But, we held our tongues and said nothing negative about the church. We just kept having our Sunday night services in the garage.

One Sunday night in the spring of 1980, a Hispanic couple drove up in our driveway. They were very well-dressed and the lady was beautiful.

They came into the garage and sat on the last row of chairs.

As I started into the message—I was preaching about the miracles of Jesus—the Lord stopped me and said, *There is one here with a terminal illness and I want to heal him.*

I really didn't understand what the word "terminal" meant, but I stopped and said, "There's someone here who has a terminal illness and God wants to heal you."

Then the Hispanic lady stood and said, "That's my husband. He has an inoperable brain tumor."

She went on, "We have a lovely home in Colonies North in San Antonio. We have three businesses and I am an officer in Frost Bank. But, everything we have means nothing now because Hector has this brain tumor that the doctors tell us is inoperable."

They came down to the front where I was standing

behind the little box I was using as a pulpit, and I asked him, "Do you believe that God can heal?"

He answered, "Well, we're Catholics, but I believe."

I told him, "That's all God asks—that you have faith to believe." Then I laid my hands on him and, although they were perfectly dry, it felt as if hot oil was running out of them.

I prayed for him.

Then the couple went back and sat down in their chairs until the service was over.

The following Sunday they came back. They drove in, parked the car, and got out. This time they ran into the garage and announced, "You won't believe what happened; you won't believe this!"

"What are you talking about?" I asked them.

Hector related, "I've been back to my doctor. They did another scan. They can't even find scar tissue on my brain where the tumor was."

"We're leaving our church and we're going to go to the hospitals and pray for the sick."

Both of them had been miraculously turned on to God.

A few months later I noticed that a little car had turned into the driveway and stopped. An old man got out and went to the trunk and took out a wheelchair. He brought it around to the passenger side and struggled to help a woman into the chair.

When he finally got her in the chair, he rolled her into the garage where we were already singing. As I started the preaching, the Lord stopped me and said, *I want to heal that woman.*

I looked at the woman and noticed how swollen her

ankles were. She looked as if she had been in that wheelchair for a long time. I wanted to make doubly sure that the Lord had spoken to me, so I turned to a man sitting with me who had come out of the Lutheran church. I told him, "Brother Jachade, the Lord wants to heal that woman in the wheelchair."

He reassured me, "Go ahead."

"I think both of us need to pray for her," I told him.

We went back to her and I said, "Ma'am, the Lord wants to heal you."

"He wants to do no such thing," she said. "I have been in the Methodist church all my life. I'm a Sunday School teacher, and not only that, I'm a public school teacher in Stockdale High School. I've been like this for sixteen years. My husband had to take early retirement from Kelly Air Force Base to care for me. We heard about your garage services and we just came to see what was going on."

I questioned her, "Would you let me pray for you?"

She looked up at her husband who was looking down at her. He said pleadingly to his wife, "We've tried everything else, why don't we let him pray for you?"

Although I wasn't sure if she agreed, I laid hands on her. I thought she was going to jump up, but she didn't move.

I had read the scripture, Acts 3:1–8, where Peter and John were going to the temple and passed by a lame man who lay at the gate which was called Beautiful. Peter prayed for the man and reached down and took him by the hand and lifted him up and told him, "In the name of Jesus Christ of Nazareth, rise up and walk."

I hesitated to pull on the lady, so I stretched out my little finger to her and she put her little finger on my little finger where there was no strength and I said, "In the name of Jesus Christ of Nazareth, rise up and walk."

She started to come up out of her wheelchair. Her husband started shouting, "She can't walk! She can't walk! I take her to her bed; I take her to the potty; she can't do any thing."

But, she kept coming up and she said to him, "Move back out of the way." Then she and I walked all over the garage.

When the little service was over that night, her husband folded up the wheelchair and pushed it out to the car. She walked to the car, got in the chauffeur's side and they drove off.

The woman had been healed by the power of Jesus Christ. They faithfully attended our services over four years until the woman died.

Double Dip Baptisms

Then they that gladly received his word were baptized...
Acts 2:41

Early in the spring of 1980, I still hadn't been baptized. At a Sunday morning service I asked the pastor of the Alamo Revival Center if he would baptize me and he said, "Sure," excitedly. "I'll be happy to baptize you. Since next Sunday is Easter, why don't we wait until then?"

I did not share this with Ruby, but on the way home, she asked, "When are you going to be baptized?"

Amazed, I said, "I'm going to be baptized on Easter Sunday."

Without hesitation, she said, "Well, I want to be baptized, too."

"Are you sure, Ruby?" I asked.

"Bill, the Bible says he that believeth and is baptized shall be saved. I believe. I want to be baptized with you."

The next Sunday night, on Easter, we were both baptized. And, thanks be to God, Ruby began to really see the miracles, and the signs and the wonders of God. She had accepted Jesus into her heart.

At one of our services we had a visiting evangelist. As he was praying for the people, a lady of the church, Sister Oma, went to our son, Billy, who was now twelve years old. She asked, "Son, do you want the Holy Spirit?"

Of course, Billy said he would like that.

So she got behind him and was pushing him by the shoulders, down to the evangelist. But, Ruby reached out and grabbed for him.

At this time Ruby did not understand about the Holy Spirit. She also did not know Billy would need It, or maybe she was afraid that he would get It.

Sister Oma just turned so Ruby couldn't reach him. And when Sister Oma and Billy reached the evangelist, before he could lay hands on Billy, our son was filled with the Holy Spirit.

On the way home that night, Ruby was telling me that she, too, had been filled with the Holy Spirit.

I couldn't believe it. "Ruby, you didn't get the Holy Ghost; I didn't hear you speak in tongues."

She insisted, "Bill, I'm telling you something hot came all over my body. I'm telling you that I got the Holy Ghost."

I still was not convinced. "Ruby, I'm sorry, but you didn't get the Holy Ghost. When you get the Holy Ghost, you'll speak in tongues." I didn't want to hurt her. I knew so much and yet hardly knew anything about what God would do, but I also knew she had felt something that night.

The next Sunday, after the service, Sister Oma asked us if we would like to go to a camp meeting. I thought, *Well, we could probably go; we could get someone to fill in for us.* I asked her about the details.

"Oh, we'll be gone about four days. It is in Tulsa, Oklahoma," she said. We agreed that it would be exciting to go with some different people and to do something out of the ordinary.

Later, as we were thinking about what we should take to go camping, Ruby said, "We don't even have a tent."

I replied, "Aw, we'll probably just take a few pots and pans. We'll probably be on a river somewhere."

Finally, Ruby called Sister Oma and asked if we should take some pots and pans—or what? And she told sister Oma that we didn't have bed rolls.

Sister Oma laughed and told her, "Everything will be set up—you don't need to take any of those things."

She added, "My niece works for Kenneth Hagen—and that's where we'll be going."

Neither of us had ever heard of Kenneth Hagen; we knew nothing about his organization.

When we arrived at the large auditorium in Tulsa, there were about 15,000 people singing and praising the Lord. We found seats in the balcony section.

As they continued to sing and praise, I heard a voice close to me singing in a beautiful language. I did not try to see whose voice it was; I just knew that it was beautiful.

We stayed the four days. It was wonderful.

On the drive home I began to relive the whole experience. I hadn't known there were that many spirit-filled people in the world. We had never been in anything like that.

Then I remembered the singing after we went in and I began thinking, *My son was sitting to my left and Ruby was sitting on my right side. That's where that singing was coming from.*

As I drove along, I asked, "Ruby, was it you doing that singing in that foreign language?"

She looked back at me and smiled, "I told you I had the Holy Ghost."

That made a believer out of me. I didn't know everything I thought I did.

A few days later, I was thinking about the wonderful things the Lord had done for me. He had lifted me out of all that sin and He had healed my body. As I thought about this, I said, "Lord, if you had a mountain large enough that I could get on it and tell the world about you, I'd do it."

I had never felt such love and peace in all my life. I wanted to do something for the Lord.

About a week had passed when Jackie Mitchum, the guest coordinator for the 700 Club out of Virginia Beach, Virginia, came into our restaurant.

She was in La Vernia visiting her ex-husband and his mother. (They shared joint custody of a child.) She was coordinating a major show in Dallas. Since she was so close she decided to fly to San Antonio and come on out to La Vernia.

Jackie, her ex-husband, and his mother had just come from Sunday morning service in the church we once attended. Ruby's cousin had invited her to come over to the restaurant and meet us.

He introduced Jackie to Ruby and made the remark, "She believes like you and Bill."

Ruby cried out, "Well, praise the Lord."

They sat down and Ruby began to tell her my testimony.

(I had been speaking at some Full Gospel business-men's meetings in several local hotels—mainly in San Antonio and Seguin.)

Jackie inquired, "Do you think your husband would come to the 700 Club and give his testimony?"

Ruby and I had never heard of the 700 Club, but Ruby said, "Well, I guess so. He's been speaking at some hotels at Full Gospel Businessmen's meetings."

They visited awhile and Jackie left.

Within a week's time we received a large envelope in the mail. It had 700 Club on it. When we opened it, we found several pages of an application to fill out to appear on the Club.

As I read through the application, I noted that a significant amount of information was required. One of the requirements was to obtain a statement from the doctor declaring that I was healed of the brain tumor.

I read about two pages, folded it up, and put it back in the envelope. "That's not God. You don't have to fill out all this paperwork to speak for the Lord." (I hadn't been required to do anything like that in the Full Gospel Businessmen's meetings.)

I just threw it on the mantle of our fireplace and it lay there for another week or so.

Somehow our testimony got into a Houston newspaper, and the people I had helped with their horses when I was quite young had seen the story.

These spirit-filled people, the Baskins, had lived just down the street from us. I had almost forgotten them; I hadn't seen them in years.

When they read that newspaper, they decided to drive to La Vernia and see if this person was that same little

Billy Moore that used to take care of their horses—and whose mother used to come to their house and pray with them.

I recognized them as they drove up in the driveway.

I invited them into the den and I shared with them that I had told God just the other day that if He had a mountain large enough I would get on the top of it, and I'd tell the whole world what He had done for me.

As the conversation continued, Mrs. Baskin looked over at the mantle of the fireplace and saw the white envelope that had 700 on it. She said, "Oh, praise the Lord, you are a member of the 700 Club."

I said, "No, ma'am, I don't know what kind of club that is. They want me to fill out a mound of papers so I can go there and speak."

"Bill, don't you know what that is?" she asked.

I answered, "No."

She said, "It's your mountain. It goes out to eighty countries around the world. It is national television, but it is owned by Christians. I'm going to help you fill out the application and you'd better send it off."

A week after I had mailed it, Jackie Mitchum called.

"Bill," she said, "we were at the round table in the conference room where all the mail is read. Ben Kinchloe, Pat Robertson, and a group of staff members were ready to read the requests.

"Pat Robertson reached into the pile and picked up an envelope. When he had finished reading it, he looked at me and said, 'Get that man from Texas here as quickly as you can.'"

Jackie went on, "Sometimes it takes three or four months to process an application, but Pat, himself, got your letter and told me to get to get in touch with you. He wants you here as soon as possible."

But," I said, "Ruby won't fly."

"That's all right," she told me. "Everything will be paid. You can drive."

Just a week before, we had bought a brand new car, so we decided to "break it in" by taking a trip to Virginia Beach.

Jackie had reserved rooms for us at the Omni Hotel. The next morning we went to the television station and I went on the set.

Pat was interviewing me, and we were about five minutes into my testimony when he was given a signal that five men from China had arrived at the television station.

These were men that Pat had been working with to arrange for Christian broadcasting into China.

He shortened our testimony and brought these Chinese men on. We were very disappointed, as was Jackie. We drove back to La Vernia.

A Building From God

Go up to the mountain, and bring wood, and build the house; and I will take pleasure in it, and I will be glorified, saith the Lord.
Haggai 1:8

About a week after our trip to the 700 Club, God woke me up about three o'clock in the morning, three mornings in a row, and showed me a building on the corner of our property. I was to build a church.

It was the same corner my mother had pointed out when I first moved her down to live with us. She had said it would be a "wonderful place for a prayer meeting."

It wasn't what my mother had said, but it was that the dream was so real; the building was so real, that I knew it was of God.

I didn't share it with my wife. I thought maybe we were going too fast and she might not agree.

Finally, I just had to tell her. "Ruby," I said, "I have to tell you about the dream I've had at three a.m. three mornings in a row. The Lord woke me each time."

She looked at me and said, "Let me tell you your dream. The Lord wants you to build a church on the corner of our property."

I was amazed and asked, "How did you know?"

She answered, "Bill, at three o'clock in the morning for three mornings, we would meet each other going to the kitchen or the bathroom. I also had dreams in which the Lord showed me a church."

Now, I knew it had been the Lord speaking to me, because we were in total agreement.

Soon we started the building. We poured the foundation in the spring of 1980.

The attendance at our services in the garage had been averaging about thirty-five people. I hadn't received any offerings because I didn't want people to think that I was using the services as another business. But, one Sunday night an elderly woman walked up and gave me a five dollar bill.

I refused. "Ma'am, I can't take that money."

But she insisted, "Oh, yes, you will. You haven't been taking tithes and offerings and you're not going to cheat me out of a blessing." Then she added, "You'd better start letting the people be blessed."

I had thought I was letting them be blessed by not taking their money. We had $8,000 in our account. That was enough to pay the contractor for a forty by seventy foot slab. So, the foundation was poured.

From that time, everything fell into place. We didn't borrow money. The Lord was putting the building together.

It was a miracle how people we didn't even know helped. A man from the oilfield pipe and supply company had a crew of electricians. He volunteered to have his men put in the electricity.

One Saturday Bill and I were working by ourselves.

We had reached a point where we were ready to start work on the inside.

I was planning to put sheet rock on the ceiling and was measuring rafters to see how it was all going to fit when Bill asked me, "Dad, what are you doing with that two by four up there?"

I replied, "I'm measuring these rafters to see how much sheet rock it is going to take."

But to my surprise, he said, "You are not going to put sheet rock in here; you need an acoustic ceiling."

Bill was only fourteen years old, but he explained, "Acoustic ceiling is good for sound."

I resisted, "Bill, I know nothing about acoustic ceiling, but I know how to put up sheet rock, so that's probably what we'll put in here."

My son reassured me, "Dad, you don't have any faith. I can put acoustic ceiling in here."

I responded by saying, "You get down here and sweep up the sawdust. I'll take care of these rafters."

He turned and went down toward the back of the church.

I heard someone drive up and I looked toward the front door, which was only an opening at that time. I saw a car drive in and park and four Hispanic ladies got out. They were dressed very fashionably, wearing high heels and hose.

Two of them walked around one side of the building and two around the other. When they got back to the front, they came in and walked back to where I was.

One of them asked, "What are you doing with those two by fours nailed together?"

"I'm checking to see if the rafters are true, so that I can put up some sheet rock."

"Surely you're not going to put sheet rock in this beautiful place," she said. "You need acoustic tile."

I heard myself say, "Yes, ma'am, but I wouldn't want to overload God." And I kind of laughed.

As they started to leave the hair on my arms was standing up. I didn't know exactly what it was, but something was different about these women.

I asked the last one of them who stepped out of the building, "Are you filled with the Holy Spirit?"

She turned and gave me a pretty smile and said, "All four of us have the Holy Ghost."

They climbed into their car and drove away.

When I arrived home from work the next Monday, I went into the church building to do some work. I found a large scaffold in the middle of the floor. There was a nice looking man on top of it.

"What are you doing up there?" I asked.

He looked down and said, "Hi, brother. I'm measuring this ceiling to see how much acoustic tile it's going to take."

When asked the cost of installing acoustic tile in here, he said, "Nothing brother; when I left San Antonio the Lord told me to come out here and put it in for nothing."

As it turned out, he was the brother of the four women who had been there on Saturday. He was an acoustic tile contractor in San Antonio. Like his sisters, he, too, was spirit-filled.

The women had gone back to San Antonio and told him that there was a man who was building a church on the highway out of La Vernia. They thought he should come out here and put in the ceiling for that man.

One miracle after another took place. The little church

building was raised up and completed. When it was finished, it was all paid for and we hadn't borrowed a dime. God had put that building together debt-free.

Then, the question arose as to what we would call the church. I hadn't thought about that, but I didn't want it to be a common religious name.

I asked Sister Oma of the Alamo Revival Center what I should do about the name. She replied, "First, you need to get a lawyer and a tax exempt number."

She informed me that there were some legalities that had to be taken care of—something that I hadn't even thought about, although we had businesses. I guess I thought this was different.

Sister Oma told me of a spirit-filled lawyer in San Antonio. When I visited this man, he gave me by-laws and a constitution, and he arranged for the preparation of the paperwork. I asked what I owed him, to which he responded, "I generally get 500 dollars, but if God tells you not to pay me anything, you don't owe me a dime."

The Lord hadn't told me not to pay him, so I paid him the 500 dollars and now we had a tax exempt number. But, I still hadn't come up with a name for the church.

"Now," he said, "you've got to have a name."

Something just rose up in my spirit and, without thinking, I said, "What about La Vernia Christian Teaching Center?"

He agreed saying, "That doesn't sound too religious. I think it's a good name; I'll put that through." So, he did all the paperwork and within a short time we received our tax exempt number and had everything done to fill the requirements with the State of Texas and the IRS.

We were now in the church business, but more importantly we were in business for the Lord.

Sell Out—Serve Me

A wise son maketh a glad father…
Proverbs 10:1

Our son, Bill, at the age of thirteen years, was a great help to us in leading praise and worship in our garage services. When we moved into the new church building, he continued helping with the services and also taught the Bible to the young children.

When he was fifteen, he went to his high school principal and asked if he could hold Bible studies at the school, and he was allowed to do so.

Although he was persecuted by some of the older students, he continued to teach eighty to ninety students regularly in the library. But, one day, the principal called him into his office and told him he would have to discontinue the classes.

He said although some of the students were gaining spiritual truths and some of their lives seemed to be changing, a lot of parents were upset and wanted the classes stopped.

Bill had heard about other schools having a "Fifth Quarter"—that was after the ball games when the students would gather in a park, or some other place where they would listen to different speakers. He asked the principal if he would open the gate which led out of the ball field into the city park so he could hold a "Fifth Quarter" there after the Friday night ball games.

The principal agreed, "I guess there's nothing they can say about that."

So, Bill built a float and put a band together to stand on the float to attract and entertain the students after the games. He was soon having youth rallies in the city park, attracting a large number of kids for each session.

They were having a great time praising and worshipping the Lord. Many little children and teenagers were being saved.

People would come into the restaurant asking, "Where in the world does this kid get all his knowledge of the Word of God?"

We told them that he often listened to God's Word on tape, sometimes up to one or two o'clock in the morning. Occasionally, we would go into his room and turn off the tape. It seemed he was constantly in God's Word.

Even though he was active in academics at the school, and he was also on the football team, he was even more active in getting God's word out. It was "blowing the minds" of pastors in town.

We knew that one day Bill would be doing something great for the Lord.

Even though our businesses were doing well, and I was still working at my trade, the Lord had been dealing with me for several months about going into the ministry full time.

I had been looking at the numbers attending our services. I thought, *It's not time, there're not enough people. You should not quit your job for an attendance of thirty or forty people.*

But, one morning in October of 1980, we got a phone call before I left for work. A strong wind had come through town and it had torn part of the roof off one of our storage sheds.

One of the waitresses had called early enough that I had time to go check it. When I got there I found three pieces of tin had blown off.

I brought a ladder and climbed up on top to nail the tin down. (I was supposed to be on the job at eight o'clock that morning at the HEB store we were building, but I took the time to make the repairs.)

Before I could climb off the roof onto the ladder, I became deathly ill. Somehow I managed to get down, and my wife drove around behind the café just as I was coming off the ladder.

Anxiously, she asked, "What's wrong with you?"

I answered, "I don't know. I'll be all right."

As I reached the pickup and took hold of the door handle, my knees started to buckle, so Ruby took me home. "I have to make some arrangements," she said. "When the doctor gets in, I'll take you to Seguin."

I called a prayer warrior who prayed with me. My son had not left for school, so he said, "Dad, I'll pray with you," so we prayed together. When Ruby got home I was still not feeling well, so she drove me to the doctor's office.

As we sat in one of the examination rooms, a nurse came and took my blood pressure. When she left, Ruby looked at me and said, "You know what this is all about, don't you? God wants you to go full time."

I answered, "Yeah, I know. He's been dealing with me,

but I didn't know how to share it with you. I didn't think the church was big enough."

"Bill," she insisted, "you had better go full time."

Wanting to be sure that this was what I should do, I asked, "Are you in agreement?"

"Yes, I am," she answered, and all of a sudden the spirit of infirmity, or whatever it was, left me.

When the doctor came in, he asked, "What's seems to be your problem?"

Without hesitation, I replied, "I don't think anything is wrong, Doc. Whatever my problem was, it's gone now."

He checked me over and said, "You seem to be all right." So, we left.

We drove down to a place called Green Gate, which was a nursery. It was just before Mother's Day and Ruby wanted to buy some plants for the mothers of the church.

As I sat in the car waiting for Ruby, a very large man walked up to the car. I had the window about halfway down on the passenger's side. He looked in the window and said, "It's a terrible thing to be out of the will of God." And, he walked away.

We continued on our way home and I was feeling fine.

When Bill arrived home that evening, he came in, looked at me, and said, "Dad, the Lord told me what was wrong with you this morning."

"Okay, what was wrong?"

"The Lord wants you to go full time," he said.

So, after Bill, his mother, and the tall man at the nursery spoke to me, I knew it must be God's will.

I called the company and told them I wanted to quit my job, but I wanted to give them a full two-week's notice.

The Christian owner said, "No, I don't want a Jonah on the job, and if God wants you to go full time, we'll make out."

Two months after I had left the construction work, fifteen of us were standing in a circle at prayer meeting on Friday night, when Ruby told me personally that the Lord said we were to sell our businesses.

I replied, "This is not God speaking."

"Don't you think God can speak to me, too?" she asked.

"Oh, yes," I told her, "I'm sure he can."

So, I shared with the others what Ruby had said. Then I told them that I was really going to make it hard on God. (Because I didn't think God would ask me to quit my job and sell all the businesses.) I declared, "God, we are going to need an answer before next Friday night's prayer meeting."

We all agreed that if selling the businesses was God's will, He would send a buyer. That was on Friday night.

Wednesday morning a man walked into the office and asked Ruby if it was true she was considering selling the restaurant.

She told him it was true, but everything else had to go along with it—the beauty shops, the apartments, the drive-in, and all the buildings.

He didn't bat an eye, but said, "I figured that. I just sold the Crystal Chandelier over in New Braunfels. I have some money that I have to get rid of or Uncle Sam will end up with most of it. I would like to buy the entire establishment."

By Wednesday evening we were completely out of business. We had signed the papers and now we were full-time with the Lord.

I didn't know what was going to take place, but God had it all planned out for our town and our county. He was raising up a spirit-filled church that believed in the Book of Acts and believed Mark 16:17, "And these signs shall follow them that believe; in My name shall they cast out devils; they shall speak with new tongues;"

We were believers and we were waiting on God to do what He wanted to do through us and for the community.

Miraculous Results of Yielding to God

Now unto him that is able to do exceeding abundantly above all that we ask or think, according to the power that worketh in us.
Ephesians 3:20

Ruby had always done the paperwork and managed our businesses. Now that they had been sold I was wondering what Ruby would do in the ministry.

We heard about the Accelerated Christian Education (ACE) program that was for pre-kindergarten through twelfth grade. Ruby began to seek information about it. She talked with people already involved in it and obtained their advice and help.

We ended up calling ACE headquarters in Lewisville, a town outside of Dallas. They informed us that in order for us to have an ACE school we would have to go through one of their programs. We were told that if the pastor was to be principal of this school, it was mandatory that he come to their school and go through training.

Ruby looked at me and I looked at her and I said,

"With a sixth grade education, I don't know if I could even qualify to walk in the door."

But, Bill spoke up. (This was to be his last year of high school.) He said, "Hey, that sounds great. I'd like to go to Dallas with Dad and go through that principal program."

We thought and prayed about it, and we agreed.

So, off we went to Dallas for the ACE training program. Bill came through with flying colors. And I did pass—which was a miracle of God. We were both qualified to be principals of Agape Christian Academy—which was the name we gave our school.

We started with a small group of children. Bill was our principal and Ruby was the administrator. All the training she had had over a period of years in management and keeping books really came in handy. God took what she had been doing in the world and used it to His glory in Christian education.

Now, we had a church and a Christian school. It seemed as if God had His hands behind us, pushing us into these areas.

I was still looking for a pastor to take over the church because I felt so unqualified in Bible knowledge and education. But, I was spending ten to twelve hours a day in the Word of God.

I was researching and studying; I was meditating on the Word. As I had begun to really study, it seemed that God was just pouring revelation into me that I never could have received except by the spirit of God.

One day in May of 1980, Ruby received a phone call from a woman who was a housekeeper for an ex-banker and cattleman who lived in our little town. The man had been sick for several years and had two registered nurses attending him around the clock.

This lady who called was Catholic. She evidently knew the man was near death and wanted someone to perform "last rites" for him.

I picked up a pastor who was a friend and we drove to this man's house. When we reached his upstairs room, we found ten to fifteen people gathered there.

As I walked in the door, one of the two nurses asked what I was going to do. I stated that I was going to pray for Mr. Wiseman.

But she said, "Bill, Mr. Wiseman is dead."

"Dead?" I asked.

"Yes," she said. "Come over to the bed. We are waiting for his brother to come in from Corpus Christi to make funeral arrangements. He's the guardian of the estate. We are also waiting for the Justice of Peace."

She pulled the man's arm from under the cover. It was gray in color and cold and stiff. She told me, "Bill, it is too late."

My friend, Jesse, was on the other side of the bed. We were not going to waste a trip; we were just going to pray.

As we started praying, Jesse spoke to me, "The Lord said he is going to live."

I remarked, "Well, tell them."

We turned around. The room was empty. The two nurses were standing at the door looking in and they were laughing. We finished our prayer and left.

A few weeks later I stopped downtown to put gas in my car. We had heard no report on Mr. Wiseman. The nurse who had spoken with me at his bedside walked up to me and said, "Bill, I have to apologize. We laughed and made fun of you for praying over a dead man, but an hour later, by my watch, the man sat up in his bed and asked for something to eat."

We know that he lived three more years after that. So, I think it made believers out of some people around town. I know it strengthened my faith.

Our church services were doing well. People from various denominations were coming in and going to the altar. Even with no one praying for them, they would be filled with the Holy Spirit and set free from many things hindering their lives.

One day while I was studying at home, I received a telephone call from a girl who was a teller at a bank. She wanted to know if I would pray for a lady who was in Northeast Baptist Hospital.

The teller said the woman's father had come to the bank and had withdrawn all of the money from his account. He told her that because his daughter was dying, he had relatives coming in from California. Since he did not have room in his little trailer to put them all up, he said he needed this money to help his family while they were staying in hotel rooms.

Before I could hang up the telephone, the Lord spoke to me and told me to go to the hospital and pray for this woman. Although I didn't get her name, I changed clothes and hurried to the hospital.

I didn't know who she was; I didn't know where she was, but when I got to Northeast Baptist Hospital, I went up to the second floor. There were several intensive care units in a row. I went to the first one. As I walked in I saw thirteen specialists working around a patient—the woman for whom I was to pray.

It was a strange situation. They had the bed elevated.

There were a number of machines around her with many IVs attached to her.

The team of M.D.s and interns was from the University of Texas Health Science Center. As I stood at the door I had no idea what was happening, and since it was such a strange situation, I asked God, "What should I pray for?"

The Lord spoke to me and said, *Take authority over the spirit of death and call her spirit back.*

As I walked to the head of the bed, the doctors on that side backed away, one by one. I walked up to the bed and put my hand on her head and said, "In the name of Jesus Christ of Nazareth, I command the spirit of death to come out of this woman and I call her spirit back."

When I had finished this prayer, I backed out the way I had come in. I felt as if I were out of my body. It seemed as if I were floating.

I walked to the waiting room and asked the people if any of them were relatives of the lady in the first intensive care ward. An old Hispanic man stood. He was a very stout man who had a little mustache.

He came to me and said, "That's my daughter."

I assured him, "Sir, your daughter is going to live," and I took his hand. He squeezed my hand to the point of crushing it.

He looked into my face and said, "Mister, don't lie to me. We have decided to disconnect everything within twelve hours, and we are going to let my daughter die. We brought her here several days ago and she's been in a coma ever since."

At this point, a nurse came running into the waiting room and said, "Mr. Nash, we don't know what happened to your daughter, but she just came out of the coma and she's calling for you."

He grabbed my hand again and we went down the hall. As we reached the intensive care room, he stopped.

I went in. Again, the doctors and interns backed away from the bed. I walked up and pulled the oxygen mask off one side of her face, and I said, "Thank you, Jesus."

And, in a good, strong whisper, she responded, "Thank you, Jesus."

I left the hospital and went home. I thought no more about it.

Two weeks later, this woman walked into the little church. There was a group of people with her. They were Catholics. She came and stood at the front. I had just begun to preach.

She asked, "Sir, do you remember me?"

She looked nothing like the woman in the bed with all the tubes and wires and machines. I answered, "I don't think so."

She went on, "I am the woman you prayed for at the Northeast Baptist Hospital. I had no kidneys, bladder, or vocal cords left—the lupus had taken them all away. Today, I have a new bladder, new vocal cords, and new kidneys and you healed me."

My answer was, "No ma'am, I did not heal you." I had to tell her three times that I hadn't healed her, that it was the power of Jesus Christ.

The family was saved, and they stayed with us for a number of years.

Not too long after this, a lady in town was sharing with one of our members that her husband was near death in the Floresville Hospital. She had been informed by the doctor to call in the children and relatives, that he probably would not make it through the night.

The woman had called her pastor (who was in one of the main line churches) and this pastor had told her, "I'm not going to pray for a dying man. If the doctors have already given him up, there is nothing that I can do."

So our church member told her, "Well, my pastor will go pray for him. Why don't you call him?"

When the woman called my house, Ruby talked with her. And when I returned home, Ruby told me about the lady's request for me to go and pray for her husband. However, I did not go that night and the next day was Saturday.

I had been planning to pour concrete at the home of my friend, Brother Jesse, that morning, but as I stepped out on my back steps, the Lord stopped me, saying, *I want you to go to Floresville and pray for this man.*

So I went back in and changed clothes.

Then I drove to my friend's house. We had concrete coming at ten o'clock and another man was to help us. I told Brother Jesse, "I have to go to Floresville and pray for a man. But there is another problem; as I was driving over here, the Lord told me to take you with me."

The man who was to help us asked, "What am I going to do with the concrete?"

I replied, "If God told us to go, He'll hold the concrete."

Brother Jesse and I left for the hospital. When we arrived and found Mr. Buffman, I shared my faith with him, and he agreed to let us pray with him.

He was in very bad shape; he was suffering from emphysema and he was very pale. He was under oxygen and could barely whisper.

We prayed for him; we agreed the Lord was going to raise him up. Then the Lord told me, *He will be home in three days.* I thought for a minute—*I'm not sure what home the Lord is talking about, so I won't reveal this to Mr. Buffman just yet.*

But I shared it with my friend who was on the other side of the bed. Then, I looked at Mr. Buffman and said, "The Lord said you were going to be home in three days."

In a weak whisper, Mr. Buffman replied, "I sure hope so."

Monday, as I was cutting grass around the house, Ruby came out and said, "I just got a phone call from Mr. Buffman. He wants you to come over to his house."

When I arrived at his house I found him sitting on the front porch. There was no oxygen supply in sight. He was the color of a rose instead of like a white candlestick as he had been Saturday.

I asked how he was doing.

"I'm doing great," he said. "I feel so good since you came and prayed for me. But I had another reason for calling you. I wanted to tell you that when I left the hospital, I was told that if I ever came back, you were not to come and pray for me.

"They said that you disturbed the whole hall while you were praying."

I didn't think we had made that much commotion. But I told him, "Well, it makes no difference. You are out and you're not having to go back." We both laughed, and then he and I prayed together.

Then I suggested that he needed to go to the pastor who had refused to pray for him, and, in love, let that pastor know that "Jesus Christ the same yesterday, today, and forever" (Hebrews 13:8); that He is still a miracle-working God.

One Friday evening shortly after this, a man who had

been coming to our church occasionally came walking down the aisle toward me. He was wearing some kind of brace over his head and on his shoulders.

When he reached me, I asked, "Brother Domingo, what in the world is that thing you're wearing?"

He informed me that he had broken his neck on his way to work at five o'clock the other morning. "I hit a horse and flipped my car; it landed upside down. The doctors had to put this thing on me to make sure my neck would heal."

The brace had four pins screwed into his skull. It was fitted over the top of his head and was set on sheepskin. The sheepskin kept it from rubbing and hurting his shoulders and chest.

I was amazed at it. "Well, I've never seen anything like that. We're going to pray for you."

As I laid hands on him, I told the other people in the prayer meeting to join me in laying hands on him and trust God for a miracle.

As I prayed, Brother Domingo broke into a cold sweat, and it seemed as if he almost went into convulsions. He looked strange and was moving his shoulders.

All of a sudden, a peace came upon him and he began to smile. "Brother," he said, "the Lord has healed me. Take this thing off."

I looked at the apparatus and stepped back from him.

"Man, I'm not going to take that thing off your head," I said. "It has pins in it. I'm no doctor. You go back to your doctor in the morning. Tell him what has happened—let him take it off."

Sure enough, Saturday morning, he went back to see his doctor and told him, "Doc, I went to a prayer meeting last night and they prayed for me. I felt something moving in my neck. Now I feel great and I want you to take this thing off."

"I can't take that thing off," the doctor replied. "You'll probably have to wear it for six weeks. Your neck is still broken; it just happened. It can't be healed."

Brother Domingo said, "Doc, it's my neck. I'm paying the bill, and I promise you, my neck is healed."

The doctor relented. He called in the nurse and asked her to hold Brother Domingo's chin in one place. Then he said, "I'm just going to loosen this a bit to show you that your head will fall down on your chest if I take this off."

The doctor loosened the brace and pulled the pins out.

Brother Domingo said, "I turned and looked at the doctor, and he almost fainted because I had turned my head."

Sunday morning, Brother Domingo walked into church carrying that brace in his hand. He stood before the congregation and told the story of how he had been prayed for on Friday night. He told that on Saturday, the doctor verified by examination and x-rays that his neck was completely back to normal and there was no problem.

This was just one more miracle God performed to show us that He is everything we were preaching; He is everything the Word of God tells us He is. We had faith to believe. Hebrews 13:8, "Jesus Christ the same yesterday, and today and forever."

Iron Men Also
Need Jesus

Come unto me, all ye that labour and are heavy laden,
and I will give you rest.
Matthew 11:28

The healing of Brother Domingo was just one of many miracles God had done—not counting all the other healings that had taken place inside the little church.

Over a few short years, the men that I had ministered to on the job—iron workers and construction hands—came to the church one by one, bringing their problems.

They had financial and marital problems and problems with their children. They came and they gave their hearts to Jesus Christ. These were hardened men who had lived sinful lives and God was beginning to really work in those lives.

Years ago, when I first was saved, there was one iron worker on the job with me who really gave me a bad time. He was a great big hunk of a guy. He could put an oxygen bottle on one shoulder and an acetylene bottle on the other and walk up a flight of stairs inside the Tower of the Americas which we were building at that time.

He was always making fun of me because of the tumor. One day he threw me to the floor of the tool house, and, in a playful manner, stuck a skill saw to my head and threatened to cut my head open to show the guys that the tumor was still there.

One Sunday night in June of 1989, the front doors of the church flew open just as we were coming out of prayer meeting and about to begin the preaching service. This same big man walked down the aisle with a beautiful red-haired woman beside him.

In a loud voice, he said, "Hey Bill, remember me?"

Surprised, I said, "Yes, I remember you, Phillips, how're you doing?"

Everything went quiet in the church.

Confronting me he continued, "This is my girlfriend—and she's got the same thing you had. Do you think God would take a tumor out of her head like He did yours?"

"Yes," I assured him, "yes, He can. God is no respecter of persons." (Acts 10:34)

I encouraged them to sit down, which they did. They had really broken up the first part of the service and the other people were laughing and talking to one another.

At the time I didn't realize that this man was still married. He still had children at home. He was having an affair with this woman who was the secretary of the iron workers local in San Antonio. As a last resort they came to La Vernia to see if God would perform a miracle for her.

As I began to preach and was about ten minutes into the message, suddenly the Lord stopped me. He said, *I want to heal this woman.*

I stopped and said, "Ma'am, the Lord wants to heal you tonight." She looked around and then she pointed to herself. I said, "Yes, ma'am, you in the red dress, come up."

She started up the aisle. My wife was sitting in the front pew and as the lady came by, Ruby stood and put her arms around the lady. She hugged her and began to minister to her. The lady broke down and cried like a baby.

After she and Ruby finished their conversation, I laid hands on her and I cursed the tumor in the name of Jesus, and I reminded the Lord, as He had cursed the fig tree and it withered and died from the root, I also was cursing this thing that was inoperable.

(I found out when the service was over that night that the doctors were planning to start a treatment on her the next morning in an effort to shrink the tumor. It involved a serum which had been developed at Southwest Research for Biomedical Research in San Antonio.)

The next morning she felt great. She thought about going to work, but then she received a call from the doctor. The voice on the line said, "Lorraine, you need to be down here. We want to start the serum process on your tumor."

She explained, "Doctor, I'm not coming in. I feel great; I have no pain. I went to a little church last night, and they prayed for me, and I believe I am healed."

He insisted, "Lorraine, it has deadened the nerves and that's why you don't feel any pain—because you are in the last stages of this brain tumor. You need to come in."

Obediently, she went to the doctor where several x-rays were taken. A few minutes later, the receptionist came into the waiting room saying, "Lorraine, get in here quick."

Excitedly, she jumped up and ran into the doctor's office. He had the x-rays under the light in the wall.

He explained to her, "Lorraine, this was last week. The

tumor was the size of an avocado seed. Today, we have a black-eyed pea."

By the end of the week, the tumor was gone.

The next Sunday, Lorraine came back to our church with the iron worker. This time they were accompanied by the business agent and two other iron workers. They went to the altar and gave their hearts to Jesus.

That was another one of God's miracles—not only to heal a brain tumor, but to bring souls into the kingdom of Jesus Christ.

Years later, I was asked to go to the hospital and pray for a lady. While I was there the lady introduced me to a male nurse as "A pastor from La Vernia."

The nurse asked, "What church do you pastor?"

I answered "A little interdenominational church called La Vernia Christian Teaching Center."

"Do you remember a redhead named Lorraine, the secretary for the iron workers' union?" he asked.

"Certainly," I said. "That was years ago."

He continued, "I saw her the other day. She's still healed and doing great. We had a nice little conversation."

I was filled with thanksgiving. "Praise God! She's still healed by the power of Jesus Christ. Amen."

As the church and school continued to grow, we had need of more classrooms, so I built a two-story building.

One day I was upstairs working on the air conditioner ducts and the air handler when I heard someone coming up the stairs. I was lying in a closet working on the duct and as I looked out, I could see four feet.

I crawled out and found a couple named Evans standing there. They were friends and I knew they were in the trucking business.

As he pulled up his t-shirt I saw, under his arm protruding from his rib cage, a lump about half the size of a grapefruit.

Quietly, he said, "Bill, it looks like I'm going to have to give up our home, our trucking, and everything."

He continued, "This is a malignant tumor. I've been to the doctor and he said that part of my lung will have to be removed. In addition, I will lose some of my ribs. Because we heard you preach, we went into the trucking business. You said that God wanted to prosper us. He did, and we were doing great—now it all seems to be over." He kept talking on about the bad things and what the doctors had told him.

Finally, I told him, "Mr. Evans, shut your mouth. We are not going to believe what the doctors say; we are going to believe God's report."

Mr. Evans was a very tall man. I reached up and laid my hands on him and cursed that tumor as I had cursed others in the name of Jesus and we prayed together and believed God would heal him.

He went back to the doctor a week later and the doctor was amazed. He took Mr. Evans before a number of interns at the hospital where he was teaching and showed them the x-rays. Now the tumor was completely gone.

The news went out everywhere that God had performed another miracle. The story was even published in the truckers' magazine, which was sent out all over the United States.

That has been a number of years ago. To this day, the tumor is gone. Mr. Evans is completely healed.

Demons Dealt With Here

And these signs shall follow them that believe; In my name shall they cast out devils; they shall speak with new tongues;
Mark 16:17

One Sunday evening in the spring of 1982, a friend of mine, Fred Erwin, Dean at International Bible College of San Antonio, came into our services. He brought with him a man and wife who had a ministry in Mexico and who had worked with him several nights on the streets of San Antonio with young people.

Fred had a place called the Catacombs under the Majestic Theater where he ministered to college students and other young people. They could have refreshments and food, but they were also given the Gospel and asked to accept Jesus as their personal Savior.

He had brought this couple to our church that evening because the woman had complained of a severe bladder problem. Fred had told her there was a pastor out in La Vernia who had been used by God many times in healing.

As they came into the service, I recognized my friend and asked if he would come up and give a word of testimony. He agreed, but he also wanted this couple to take part.

They gave their testimony. The woman sang a few songs and appeared very spiritual. When the service was over and people were leaving, we started out the door. Fred suddenly remembered the reason that they had come was to pray for this woman.

He said, "Brother Moore, she has a bladder problem and she needs healing."

I turned back and went to the front of the church to get oil to anoint her as in James 5:14. She had followed me and was at the altar as I turned and stretched my hand toward her. Just before I touched her, she fell flat on her back on the floor and began to crawl like a snake.

Fred said, "My Lord! She is demon-possessed." We began to minister to her, attempting to cast out the devil. We got on our knees beside her; her husband was just standing there.

Fred began to curse the demon that was in her and to work with her. This was my first experience with demons. After several hours, my wife called to see what we were doing that was keeping us so long.

I explained to her, "We're delivering a lady who is demon-possessed."

During this time, this young lady, who had been beautiful, seemed to turn into an animal. Her face contorted; her teeth seemed to protrude; she was completely different; she was ugly.

As Fred worked with her, he commanded the spirits to come out. After several hours she had been totally set free.

Then he told us we needed to take her into an inner healing. He began to take her backward in time, saying, "There's a tunnel I want to take you through. In this tunnel you will see pictures of life. There will be good pictures and there will be bad pictures. The Lord will remove the bad pictures of your life."

The lady began to go back into the tunnel; she began to see the pictures and her face showed horror. Then, as she went further in the spirit, her face would lighten up and glow. She began to describe the things she was seeing from her past life.

It was an amazing experience to listen to her. When we reached the crux of the matter, it seemed this lady's grandmother was a witch. Her mother had also been involved in witchcraft and when this poor woman was a child, she had entered her mother's bedroom and found the mother with a butcher knife in her stomach. Her mother had committed suicide.

As Fred took her back in time, he was seeking her deliverance and helping her to receive inner healing. She was totally delivered that day.

I had another experience all on my own. About two o'clock one morning, I was awakened by the telephone. When I answered, the voice at the other end said, "I need to talk to you. I want you to come to my house as soon as you can."

After talking to this person I learned that he was a rancher and sheet metal contractor that I only knew by sight. I also knew his name because he had eaten at our restaurant several times. I asked for directions to his house.

However, as I was going to the car, a strange feeling came over me and something in my spirit spoke and warned, *Take a weapon with you.*

I went back into the house wondering, *What kind of weapon?* Ruby was waiting in the kitchen, "Bill, I don't feel good about this. I don't think this is a sick call."

"I don't either," I told her. "I don't know what it is." As I looked on the counter, I saw my Bible. I picked it up and told Ruby, "The Lord told me to take a weapon; I guess this is about the best weapon I can take."

So, armed with my two-edged sword, my Bible, I drove to the ranch. When I drove into the yard, there were floodlights on all over the place.

I went to the front door and rang the doorbell. I waited, but there was no response. Then, I walked around the house to the patio. There was a large glass sliding door leading into a den.

Looking in, I could see a man sitting in a recliner. In front of him was a coffee table upon which were at least six bottles of some type of alcohol—either vodka or gin. Most of them were empty.

I called his name as I pushed open the sliding door. He did not respond, so I went in and sat in front of him in another large chair.

Then he spoke, "Oh yeah, they're out there. Listen, listen, do you hear them?"

I answered, "No, I don't hear anybody."

"Oh, yeah," he repeated, "they're out there; they're coming for me. Can't you hear them? I've already run them off one time, but they're coming back."

As he reached under the pillow he was sitting on, he pulled out a 357 magnum, shouting, "I'm going to start with you."

He pointed the gun at my face, cocked the hammer back, and I could see that all the chambers were full. I was only about five feet away from him. I looked down the barrel and said, "I rebuke you, you foul spirit. In the mighty name of Jesus of Nazareth, I command you out."

And, as I began to confess him to Jesus and to rebuke the powers of Satan, he fell on the floor. The gun was still cocked, but it slid across the floor as he fell on his knees.

And, as he stood up, he looked at me and I saw he was different—he was sober. He said, "My parents came from Houston." And he opened up a Bible—a large family Bible and pointed to Hebrews 6:4–6, "For it is impossible for those who were once enlightened, and have tasted the heavenly gift, and were made partakers of the Holy Ghost, And have tasted the good word of God, and the powers of the world to come, If they shall fall away, to renew them again to repentance; seeing they crucify to themselves the Son of God afresh, and put him to an open shame."

I asked him, "Have you accepted the Lord Jesus Christ? Have you been filled with the Holy Spirit?"

His answer was, "No."

"Then that scripture doesn't refer to you," I told him. "You must be running from God."

He continued, "My parents were from a main line denomination, and when I was young, they told me that I was supposed to be a missionary. But, I never did heed the call; I've been running; I've been making money. I have a lot of things, but I've rejected serving God. My parents came to visit and called that scripture to my attention, saying that there was no more hope for me. Then they drove back to Houston. "I've been drinking and drinking," he said. "This demon has got hold of me. I even shot four of my neighbor's best cows. I drove my bulldozer off into my stock tank. A man came to help pull me out, and I chased him down the road with my gun—and I am going to kill you if you don't help me."

I began to minister to him, and about four o'clock in the morning, he had a breakthrough. At six o'clock I thought everything was all right, and I left him.

But, three years later, I was called to preach his funeral. He had taken his own life. He had taken that 357 magnum and put it to his head, and put another gun to his stomach, and had pulled both triggers. That tells me that demons are real; that his demon had possessed his mind and his body.

John 10:10 says: "The thief cometh not, but for to steal, and to kill, and to destroy: I am come that they might have life, and that they might have it more abundantly."

One day in June 1990, I received a telephone call at my home from a lady who was calling from the hospital over in Floresville. "Pastor Moore, we watch you on cable over here. We heard you talking about casting out demons. My brother is here in the hospital. I believe he must have a demon because he is growling and foaming and he is biting the nurses. They had to give him a sedative to put him out. He plays with a group called the Blind Sacrifice. We were told that they worship Satan and that they were practicing, burning candles, and worshipping Satan when a shadow came up over the corner of the garage where they were. The thing got into his chest and he fell to the floor. He was paralyzed. They called EMS who came with the police and picked him up. Now he is here in the hospital. Would you come and see what you can do?"

I drove to Floresville and as I entered the hospital, a lady met me in the hall and asked me if I was a case worker. She was the supervisor of the hospital.

"No," I said, "I am a pastor."

She explained, "We have a man down here who is fighting and growling like an animal and biting everybody.

He is sleeping now because we gave him a shot, but we don't know what to do with him."

I went down the hall and looked in on him. A lady came to me and said, "That's my brother. Can you do something?"

"Not here," I said, "but if he is ever released, let me know, and we will come to him and the Lord will deliver him."

A few days after, when the hospital attendants still couldn't do anything with the man, they decided to move him to St. Rose on the north side of San Antonio. They told his sisters that they were going to have an ambulance take him to the emergency room at St. Rose.

Not having money for an ambulance, the sisters begged the hospital to let them take him. "We will take him if you'll let us," they said.

So, it was agreed that the sisters could transfer him, but instead of taking him to St. Rose, they brought him to the church.

I had just driven up and school was letting out. As parents were driving in and picking up their children, this woman got out of her car and said, "Brother Moore, where do you want me to put my brother?"

Not recognizing her, I asked, "What are you talking about?"

She reminded me, "The one who was in the hospital—we have him in the car. We want you to deliver him."

Then it dawned on me who they were and I suggested that they take him around to the side door.

I stopped by the office and turned in some bills and some items I had bought. Then, I went into the church where the women—one on each side were—dragging their brother.

He was paralyzed from the neck down, both arms, both legs, and his head was turned back—straight back. His face looked horrible.

As he lay on the floor, I began to minister to him and to call the spirits out of him. I commanded Satan and the demons out of him. After working with him about two and a half hours, his sisters called his mother to come from San Antonio.

When she came in, she looked at him and said, "That is not my son." She was upset because they had called her all the way out to La Vernia. She repeated, "That is not my son."

"Mama," they persisted, "this is your son. He is demon-possessed and that is why his face looks all messed up. That is why you don't recognize him."

She began to cry so they took her away to the office. I worked another four or five hours with him.

Finally, he was completely delivered. His paralysis left; his head was straight; and his tongue which had been hanging out of his mouth went back in.

Then he began to sing. His family said that he had never been to church, but he sang "Amazing Grace"—as beautifully as you have ever heard. We worked with him a little more that day. He never returned to his rock group and he became one of our members, playing the bass for our church.

I saw him recently; he was still set free and in his right mind. Nothing but the power of Jesus Christ can do these things. I thank God for the experience.

Late one evening a man knocked on the door of my den. He was tall and lanky. I knew him and invited him in. As he sat down in a chair across from mine, he began to hiss like a snake.

I could tell he was under the influence of alcohol and drugs. As he stared at me he began to glow; a very ugly look came into his eyes. He stood up and started toward me with his hands reaching out to choke me.

There was nothing I could do except to put my finger between his face and my face and rebuke him in the name of Jesus. I began to call the spirit out of him, "You unclean, foul spirit, I rebuke you in the name of Jesus. I bind you." Immediately the Lord picked him up and dropped him to the floor, and laid him horizontally in front of me.

My son, Bill, was in his bedroom, studying, and he ran in to see what was going on. As this man lay on the floor, flat on his back, he reached out his arm and grabbed Bill by the ankle and twisted it, saying, "I am going to kill you!"

My son rebuked him in the name of Jesus. The man released his ankle and he went rolling rapidly across the floor until he hit the wall, then he came up sober.

He looked at us and wanted to know what had happened. "What am I doing here?" he asked.

"The Lord has set you free," I told him.

I found out later that he had come to our house from the house of an old friend. His friend had not been at home, and this man had pulled his friend's sixty-five-year-old mother off her porch and raped her in her front yard.

When he later came to trial, the jury consisted of eleven women and one man. The District Attorney was trying to get him sentenced to twenty to twenty-five years and told the jury, "If you don't convict this man and send him to prison, he will rape all of you, and probably all of your children. This man has to be put away."

A man from AA was called to be a witness. He was the president of the San Antonio chapter.

He was asked, "What is your occupation?"

"I am president of the AA organization in San Antonio," was the answer.

The prosecuting attorney then asked, "Are you an alcoholic?"

He answered, "I am a recovering alcoholic?"

Then he was asked, "Are you still an alcoholic?"

"I am always struggling," he said. "I cannot touch alcohol or be around it because I'm still an alcoholic."

He was asked a few more questions and then dismissed.

Then I was called as a character witness.

The lawyer asked if I had ever drunk alcohol, to which I answered, "Yes."

He asked, "Do you think you were an alcoholic?"

"I don't know," I said, "but I probably was because I lived most of my life drinking alcohol."

The next question was, "Are you still an alcoholic?"

"No," I said, "I am no longer an alcoholic."

The lawyer continued. "So you're different from this man who is president of AA. He's still an alcoholic, and you are not. What is the difference between you and him?"

Boldly, I answered, "He went through a program, and I went through Jesus Christ. And, if this man on trial isn't totally delivered, I will serve his time in the penitentiary."

The jury went to deliberate. When they came back they gave him a ten year probated sentence. He spent not one day in jail. Ten years later he was helping in a jail ministry, trying to bring the prisoners to Jesus.

Weird and Wonderful Happenings in Wilson County Jail

…The Lord looseth the prisoners…Psalm 146:7

My own jail ministry came about as the result of a horrible crime spree.

On November 3, 1983, Pete S. and his nephew, Leroy, were out drinking. They drove to La Vernia and stopped their car on a country road. The deputy sheriff drove by and they flagged him down.

Sam Childress stopped his patrol car to render aid. They surprised him by holding a gun in his face.

After taking off his badge and his shirt, they secured his hands behind his back with his own handcuffs and stuffed him into the trunk of the patrol car and shot him.

They closed the trunk lid and drove the patrol car into town and robbed the La Vernia State Bank.

Then they drove back to their own car on the country road, got out, raised the trunk lid, and found Sam Childress still alive. Then they shot him again, got into their own car and drove off to San Antonio.

A little over a week later, the FBI caught up with them. After booking them for murder, they were brought out to Wilson County and put in jail.

Sheriff Bonham, who knew me from the time we were both members of the Lutheran church, called me to ask if I would come talk to these two prisoners.

"I would appreciate it if you would come over to the jail and see if you could minister to these men," he requested. "One of them has banged his head up against the iron door of the cell. He is screaming for cigarettes. I thought maybe you would come and see if you could help this guy out. He's acting really strange," the sheriff continued, "like he is full of devils, or whatever."

I went to the jail and ministered to the two killers. The jailers allowed me to enter into their separate cells. I talked with them about Jesus Christ and about deliverance.

Pete S. ended up being totally delivered from the power nicotine held over him. I told him about the healing power of Jesus, that God could heal him not only physically—but spiritually—and he accepted Jesus Christ as his Lord and Saviour.

After I worked with Pete five months, I received a tape from him pouring out his heart, letting me know he had begun to minister to other prisoners.

Although I ministered to Leroy, he did not receive the healing power of Jesus as his uncle had.

Thus, began my jail ministry.

The second Thursday night that I ministered in the jail, the Lord directed me to bind up all the demons that had taken up residence there over a period of years.

The place was full of principalities. As Paul wrote

in Ephesians 6:12, "For we wrestle not against flesh and blood, but against principalities, against powers, against the rulers of the darkness of this world, against spiritual wickedness in high places."

That night I took two brothers in the Lord with me to introduce them into the jail ministry. I told them, as we brought all the prisoners into a cage-like room large enough to hold them, "We are going to bind up the demons tonight. God is going to have liberty to minister and do what He has come to do."

I began to pray. Four or five minutes into the prayer of binding up spirits and principalities, we heard many voices that sounded as if they were coming down the hall. There was screaming and yelling, and I thought at first it might be prisoners who had not joined us. Or, I thought, it could be guards mocking and making this blood curdling screaming.

The voices went to the end of the hall where there was a large steel door that led to the exercise yard. There was no one in the hall at the time. We were even afraid to look up, but we kept praying.

When we walked by the dispatcher's office on the way out of the jail after services that night, it was full of law officers. There were some D.P.S. patrolmen and the sheriff was there with three deputies. All were in that little room where the dispatcher worked.

I waved at them and smiled, but their faces were like stone. They looked as if they were in shock.

The dispatcher told me the next week that when she had heard all the voices coming down the hall screaming and yelling, that she got on the phone and called all the law officers to come to the jail.

They could hardly believe what this woman told them.

But, we had heard it and this woman had heard it, and had even turned on her two-way radio so that the officers in their cars could hear it.

We know that God had His way that night and had taken authority over the demons.

Later, the county built a larger jail that had facilities for about 160 prisoners. We continued our jail ministry to murderers, rapists, and bank robbers—all kinds of inmates.

After the big jail was built, the federal marshals and others would rent cell space from Wilson County.

I will never forget when they brought in Robert T., a young man only twenty-five years old with fifteen murders to his credit.

He was one of the head mafia leaders in San Antonio. He had begun following his daddy's footsteps when he was a very young boy.

In order to gain recognition and get promoted in the mafia, he had to kill fifteen messed-up drug dealers who had run afoul of the mafia.

He had been given two life sentences without possibility of parole and is still in the penitentiary.

Another notable inmate was John S., a businessman who was also a con artist. He was on the board of three hospitals and he owned three catering services in San Antonio.

But, he was also a racketeer and had been caught, tried, and sentenced to thirty years in the penitentiary.

After I had been ministering at the jail every Thursday night for three months, this man came to me and said, "Okay, it takes a con artist to know one, and I thought you were one, but now I want to know this Jesus Christ."

John was saved and he began to minister to the other prisoners.

One night, he heard the sounds of weeping in the cell next to his. He began to tell the man on the other side of the wall about Jesus. The man happened to be Robert T.

Using God's word to minister to this murderer about the love and power of Jesus, John reached into Robert's heart and he was saved by the Holy Spirit.

The U.S. Marshall gave permission for me to baptize him. We brought in a cattle trough to use for this purpose. Two guards had to lift him into the water because he had to wear handcuffs and leg irons.

I also obtained permission to tape an interview with him so we could present it to children and teach them what living a life in prison would be like.

After Robert T. was saved, my wife and I went to the far west side of San Antonio and ministered to his wife and two little children.

They also accepted the Lord Jesus as Savior. My wife and I gave them Bibles.

John S. continued his preaching ministry among the prisoners. He knew more Bible than I because he had a lot more time to study the scriptures. They finally allowed him to hold services for his fellow inmates.

One important aspect and outreach of my jail ministry is that it resulted in the Floresville High School allowing us to have a rally in the high school auditorium so we could reach the young people.

I wanted to take one of the prisoners to this meeting in his jail uniform, leg irons, and hand-cuffs to make a visual impression and then let him give his testimony.

I spent time trying to decide which prisoner would be the one to take and I found just the right one.

A three-time loser was in jail at that time.

He had been a big drug pusher, had lots of money, and had spent a lot of time in the penitentiary and had ended up in the little jail in Wilson County—a notable prisoner indeed.

This man had been marvelously saved, and I thought, *Man! He would be the right guy.*

I asked the sheriff if he would allow me to take him to the big rally we would be having for the youth over at the high school auditorium. "Yes, no problem," he said.

"Well, I want leg irons and handcuffs and I want him in his uniform that you have here—his jail clothes—to make an impression."

The sheriff agreed.

The night of the rally I went to pick him up. I figured they would send at least one or two guards to drive him over to the school. I went into the jail and had to wait a few minutes; then they brought him out.

He was carrying his leg irons and handcuffs. I asked the guard, "Who are you going to send with me?"

He replied, "Nobody; if he gets away from you, he's in trouble anyhow."

I thought he was joking, but he wasn't.

The prisoner and I walked out and got into my pickup and we drove to the school. I was going to help him put on the leg irons, but I didn't know how.

"Oh," he said, "I've had them on so many times; let me put them on, I'll show you how to do it."

So, he hobbled out onto the stage and gave a great testimony of how his life had been filled with women, drugs, and money, but now had changed for the glory of Jesus Christ.

He was very impressive and a lot of children came down and gave their lives to the Lord.

So, the jail ministry has been rewarding with one testimony after another. The county jail built a large exercise room similar to a gym and would allow the prisoners to come in on Thursday nights and some began to be filled with the Holy Spirit and fall out on the floor.

One night one of the guards asked me how I knew how to hypnotize people. I told him, "Brother, this is not hypnotism. It is the power of Jesus Christ coming into these prisoners."

When we were still at the little jail we didn't have a baptismal tank like the big jail has now. We had the water trough and sometimes the sheriff would even allow me to bring prisoners over to the church to baptize them and then take them back to the jail.

To this day I still receive letters from prisoners telling me how God has changed their lives; how they went out into society and began to minister the gospel of Jesus Christ.

And God is still working in marvelous ways in the jail ministry today.

A Full Quiver

As arrows are in the hand of a mighty man; so are the children of the youth. Happy is the man that hath his quiver full of them…
Psalm 127:4, 5

I turn now from the dark side of things to a very bright spot in my life—my children. They have been a great blessing. I am thankful to my God for giving them to me.

Each of them has been successful in life in his (and her) own way and I am so proud of them. I feel shame when I think of the rocky start Norma and I provided for the older three—Billy Sam, Brenda, and Joey, but that was part of my "gutter" life before Jesus saved me and lifted me up.

I want to write about them now, one by one, oldest to youngest, and tell how they've turned out.

In the divorce proceedings, Norma (my first wife and the mother of these three children) lied to everyone, including her lawyer and the judge, claiming I had not supported the children during our separation.

When I produced all my receipts and money orders, the judge was inclined to grant me custody. He decided

Norma was not competent to raise the children. Her attitude and all the lies had not left him with a favorable impression of her.

But, I told him that I had not been exactly stable myself. I did not know what I was going to be doing; I did not know exactly where I was going. I said, "I think they need to be with their mother. At least they have a home and can go to the school where they started."

That is why I gave up custody.

Although the judge was amazed, he went along with it.

Earlier in my story, I told how I pulled strings to get my oldest boy, Billy Sam, into construction and the union. He was a good worker and climbed to the position of junior superintendent in the company that built the Astrodome in Houston. Later, I helped him get a job in the union with the Operating Engineers. He is still with them today, working for a large crane company, doing the job sites for them, and choosing which cranes are required.

Billy Sam and his wife have two sons.

Brenda went to work for a bank in Lytle, and today she is an officer in the bank. She and her husband have a son and daughter.

We helped my son, Joey, obtain a job through a friend at Southwest Research and Joey just worked his way right on up—promotions one after another. The company has sent him to install antennae wherever our Navy has ships.

He and his wife have a son and daughter.

Bill, our youngest son, and his wife have three sons.

So, we have been blessed with grandchildren as well and also have good relationships with them.

We get together every Christmas and sometimes on Thanksgiving or a birthday. By the grace of God, we have been able to keep the love and communications open between us.

From the beginning of my marriage to Ruby, the three older children loved her because she was so good to them. She loved them and treated them as if they were her own. They "took to" our youngest son, Bill, immediately when he was born.

I have related a little of Bill's story and how he was a real help to us as we started our church and school, but there's much more to tell since then.

In January of 1997, Bill left us and went to Brownsville for a two-day revival in an Assembly of God Church. The revival lasted for three months. There were healings, deliverances, and the church attendance increased from about thirty-five members to around 200.

The pastor grew jealous and upset and he closed the revival, but the people came to Bill, "You're not going back to La Vernia. We'll rent a ballroom at one of the hotels."

They did, but it was costing them a thousand dollars for a Sunday service.

After a time they were able to move to a country club which had better facilities for a little less money, and they didn't have to break down all their equipment every Sunday.

So, with God's help, they kept services going in this large auditorium until they were able to build a large facility. They named it Living Way Family Church.

Now they are averaging over 300 students in their Christian school. They've also added a large gym and a church building that's over 24,000 square feet.

Bill was prophesied over one night in Brownsville by a lady who said that God had brought him there for a specific reason—that He was going to give favor to Bill in Brownsville, McAllen, and Harlingen.

Furthermore, she prophesied that Bill would be on television, as a host for a Trinity Broadcasting Network program, and that it would come to pass that he would also cross over the border into Mexico, preaching the gospel.

These things have all come to pass in his ministry and it is growing day by day. God is using him to do wonderful works for the Lord Jesus Christ.

God Said Build and We Built

Except the Lord build the house, they labour in vain that built it…
Psalm 127:1

In 1995 after we had spent fifteen years in our original building, I began to feel the Lord was directing me to build a larger sanctuary, one that would seat six to 700 people. (I thought those figures strange, because our town's population was only a little over 600, and there were seven other churches in the town.)

Since I do not believe in putting my people in debt and I don't believe in pledges, I told myself, *I will just wait on the Lord.* So, I shopped around for fabricators and found one on the other side of Dallas that would deliver the building on the job site with down gutters, trim, and everything the building needed for 48,000 dollars. They wanted fifteen percent down so they could begin fabrication.

The next day, I asked the church secretary to write a check for fifteen percent of the 48,000 dollars. That would come close to bankrupting the church, but she wrote the check.

When I went to pick up the check, the father of one of our students walked into the office and inquired, "Is that for the new church?"

"It is," I said.

His response was, "Why are you going to let them rip you off?"

"This is the lowest price I have found," I said.

"Well," he said, "I just built a new building, fifty by 100 feet, for 12,000 dollars delivered onto the job site.

"But," I said, "I've already given my word, and I have the check for fifteen percent."

He kept trying to convince me, and I finally gave in. We called the company in Dallas with whom he had dealt and gave them the size of the building, 12,500 square feet. They quoted a price of 26,000 dollars.

Then I called the first company to ask if they could cut their price to match this new quote. When they said they couldn't, we went with the company with the best price.

They delivered to the job site for 26,000 dollars. This did not include erection or all the things which had to be done on the interior. But, we began the work with a few faithful members, the youth pastor, a retired insulator, my son, and me.

We didn't have a blue print or anything to go by. Every night when I went to bed, I would ask the Lord to give me directions for the next day. I have to give the Lord the glory because everything fit together, and it turned into a beautiful church building, for which we have received many compliments.

A few years later, the Lord told me that He wanted me to

build a snare. *A snare?* I asked. *Yes,* He said. *I want you to build a trap. You've been doing jail ministry for eighteen years. Why wait until these people get in jail? I want you to build a New Life Family Center, especially for the young people to use on Friday nights.*

Work with them where they can play ball—where they can have basketball and volleyball games. And I want a snack bar in it, and I want a kitchen. The Lord just seemed to speak to me out of His spirit.

Okay, Lord, I said. And I contacted the same company in Dallas. They gave me a good price on this building which was 10,000 square feet, and poured the slab.

About four o'clock on the morning we were to set the steel, it started raining. There was a man in our church who had agreed to knock his crew off a few days and help me put up the red iron.

It rained and rained, but we worked all day. The individual who had the contract became angry because we were working in the rain and refused to honor the contract on the building.

The next day, a man who had been working on the county road behind the church, and had seen us working all day in the pouring rain, walked into the office and offered his help, "I thought you might need an iron worker."

"I definitely need a connector," I stated.

He remarked, "That's what I used to do—connect iron for the big power plants."

So, he went to work and we got all the red iron up. I paid him for the first week, but he wouldn't take a dime for the next two weeks. He was an "old farm boy" and a devout Catholic. "This one's for God," he declared.

We were able to erect the whole structure for 375 dollars. That was a miracle from God. And, the other miracle was that this man showed up just at the time I needed a connector.

The ministry was very successful. We invited the children to come in every Friday night. We would have refreshments and play games, often stopping in the middle of a game to minister to them with testimonies and preaching.

This was the beginning of the New Life Family Center. Many have been saved and it is a great success today.

Get to the Nitty Gritty—It's All About Faith

So then faith cometh by hearing, and hearing by the word of God.
Romans 10:17

We are still seeing our share of miracles and healings at La Vernia Christian Teaching Center. The most recent that occurred involved one of the ladies in the choir. She came down when we gave the Sunday morning altar call.

"I have a tumor," she told me. She raised her skirt to her knee. "It is growing and giving me a lot of pain. I believe that God is going to remove this thing."

We prayed God would remove the tumor and I laid hands on her. When I finished praying, she returned to her seat, about four rows from where we were standing for the altar call.

Before she sat down, she felt of her knee and called

out, "The tumor is gone—completely! There is no more tumor!"

"Isn't that the reason you came down here?" I asked. "Didn't you tell me that God was going to perform that miracle for you?"

The whole assembly laughed. She rejoiced and we rejoiced with her.

And there was a man who had colon cancer. He had taken three chemotherapy treatments which cost 1,500 dollars a shot. The doctors wanted him to keep taking them.

I said, "Brother Jim, you don't need to continue this; all it is going to do is destroy the rest of the cells in your body. God is a healer. You're going to have to have faith to tell your doctor you're stopping the chemo."

So he went to his doctor and told him he did not want any more chemotherapy.

The doctor insisted, "We're going to have to complete these treatments or the cancer will come back."

But Brother Jim said, "I'm trusting God," and took no more treatments. Several months later he went back for tests and not one trace of cancer was found in his colon. He also had been healed by the power of God.

There are many, many more of these amazing true stories that I could share, but I trust I've related enough to convince you of God's mighty power and His love for us in the name of Jesus.

I'm trusting that this word will bring *faith;* I'm trusting this book will bring *faith* to those who are struggling—and to those who are looking for God to do something in their lives.

Remember, He is no respecter of persons. What He was able to do for one, He is able to do for all.

As I look back upon my life and see God's amazing grace and patience and His never-ending love to those who are willing to deny self and take up their cross and follow Him, I realize God is not looking for super stars as Paul said in I Corinthians 1:26–31:

> For ye see your calling, brethren, how that not many wise men after the flesh, not many mighty, not many noble, are called: But God hath chosen the foolish things of the world to confound the wise; and God hath chosen the weak things of the world to confound the things which are mighty; And base things of the world, and things which are despised, hath God chosen, yea, and things which are not, to bring to nought things that are: That no flesh should glory in his presence. But of him are ye in Christ Jesus, who of God is made unto us wisdom, and righteousness, and sanctification, and redemption: That according as it is written, He that glorieth, let him glory in the Lord.

And my real testimony is as Paul said in I Corinthians 2:1–5, and in Ephesians 2:1–5:

> And I, brethren, when I came to you, came not with excellency of speech or of wisdom, declaring unto you the testimony of God. For I determined not to know any thing among you, save Jesus Christ, and him crucified. And I was with you in weakness, and in fear, and in much trembling. And my speech and my preaching was not with enticing words of man's wisdom, but in demon-

stration of the Spirit and of power: That your faith should not stand in the wisdom of men, but in the power of God.

I Corinthians 2: 1–5

And you hath he quickened, who were dead in trespasses and sins; Wherein in time past ye walked according to the course of this world, according to the prince of the power of the air, the spirit that now worketh in the children of disobedience: Among whom also we all had our conversation in times past in the lusts of our flesh, fulfilling the desires of the flesh and of the mind; and were by nature the children of wrath, even as others. But God, who is rich in mercy, for his great love wherewith he loved us, Even when we were dead in sins, hath quickened us together with Christ, (by grace ye are saved;).

Ephesians 2: 1–5